Child Labour in Hazardous Sectors

CHILD LABOUR IN HAZARDOUS SECTORS

Editor

Rabi Narayan Misra

Reader in Commerce
Science College
Hinjilicut (Orissa)

DISCOVERY PUBLISHING HOUSE
NEW DELHI-110002

First Published-2003
Reprinted - 2014
ISBN 978-81-7141-646-2

Published by
DISCOVERY PUBLISHING HOUSE
4831/24, Ansari Road, Prahlad Street,
Darya Ganj, New Delhi-110002 (India)
Phone: 3279245 • Fax: 91-11-3253475
E-mail:dphtemp@indiatimes.com

Printed at:
Infinity Imaging Systems
Delhi

Preface

Human asset is the biggest and important asset of a Nation. Child is the future citizen of the country. He is innocent and dependent. Proper care should be taken for the physical and mental development of a child to establish as a good citizen. But in India more than 40 per cent of children are due to some reasons or other forced to work in different hazardous sectors, to meet their needs as per the desire of the employers. At time, due to work in hazardous field, their health are deteriorating and causes premature death. Unless proper steps have to be taken from Government and from different NGO's and public as a whole, to change their socio-economic scenario, this fire-fighting problem can not be solved on the years to come.

This book is of immense help to planners, research scholars, Government, Non-Government Organisations and others who are thinking about economic development of the country.

Rabi Narayan Misra

Acknowledgements

I am very much thankful to all the paper contributors for touching the various aspects on Fire Fighting problems of Child Labour in Hazardous occupations. It is only possible on my part to edit this book by their kind help and Co-operation.

I am thankful to all my friends and members of the Commerce and Economics Society of Orissa, Gandhi Nagar–6, Berhampur—1, Orissa who were helped me for editing this book.

I am also thankful to my wife Swarnaprava, who has helped and co-operated with me from the various aspects for editing this book. I also thankful to my sons Roopesh Kumar and Rookesh Kumar who were helped me as and when necessary to edit the book. Their love and affection has inspired me to do this job without any problem.

It is last but not least, I am very much thankful and grateful to Sri Tilak Wasan, Proprietor, Discovery Publishing House, New Delhi, who had readily accepted my proposal in publishing this book in spite of their heavy pressure during this session. I, on behalf of all our contributors, family members, and friends thanks to all members of Discovery Publishing House, New Delhi—2 for their kind help and co-operation on publishing the book in time.

Contents

1

Child Labour in India: Some Issues

*Prof. Kishore C. Raut
**Dr. M. Kamalun Nabi
***Ms. Rajeshwari Panigrahi

Introduction

The biggest assets of a nation are its human and natural resources. The latter has to be preserved and not plundered; while the former has to be developed into complete human beings to enable them to contribute to their own welfare and to humanity as a whole. Against such avowed policy framework, one of the most abusive practices of human exploitation is found in the form of child labour in almost all the countries of the world in varying degree. There are thousands of children who have been deprived of their

* P.G. Department of Commerce, Berhampur University, Berhampur—760 007, Orissa.

** Lecturer in Commerce, R.C.M. Sc. College, Khallikote, Ganjam, 761 030, Orissa.

*** Research Scholar, P.G. Department of Commerce, Berhampur University, Berhampur—760 007, Orissa.

childhood—those lovely days of fun and frolic. They work under the scorching sun and piercing rain only to make their both ends meet. In fact, millions of children languish in slavery in dimly lit, cramped spaces in factories, houses, toiling at times upto 20 hours a day, getting little pay and more abuse—life continues as usual. Perhaps this is what destiny has in store for them. This is the grim reality of child labour and at the gateway of the 21st century, child labour continues as the worst form of slavery in the society.

Children are innocent, vulnerable and dependent. They are also active and full of hope. Their time should be one of joy and peace, of playing, learning and growing. Their future need to be shaped in harmony and co-operation. Their lives should mature as they broaden their perspectives and gain new experiences. But for many children, the reality of childhood is altogether different. Much to their dislike and distaste, youngsters find themselves in the workplace. At a time when they should be playing, they are subjected to servitude. This is a grim tale not only in Asia but also in the countries of Africa and Latin America where poverty stalks.

The Dimension

Child labour is a global phenomenon. Its magnitude and dimension however vary widely from country to country. The obnoxious practice of child labour is widely prevalent in many of the third world countries such as India, China, Pakistan, Bangladesh, Nepal, Brazil, etc. Despite various measures undertaken by the Government and the non-government agencies to tackle the exploitation of children, India has come to acquire the dubious distinction of possessing the largest child labour force in the world. According to estimates, there are over 60 million child labourers in India constituting nearly twenty five per cent of the working children of the world. Besides, Pakistan and Bangladesh account for highest percentage of child labour in the world.

Large scale employment of children in India below the age of 14 is predominantly found in glass, carpet weaving, match, fireworks, beedi, brassware, pottery, bangle industries and as domestic helpers, and also in rural industries such as construction, brick, kiln units, iron ore and red-oxide mines, tile manufacturing units, etc. Systematic destruction of rural life, menacing spread of urbanisation, commercialisation of education and the drastic cut in the budgetary allocation towards various poverty alleviation schemes, etc., are the causative factors behind the alarming spread of child labour, forced labour and bonded labour.

Interestingly, engagement of children in work conditions is not altogether a new phenomenon in India. It has been in practice since time immemorial. In the earlier days, children particularly from low-income groups were engaged in the works, which mostly comprised a part of the labour force in the agriculture and the artesian sector, within their own families. The resultant workload always allowed them to draw a distinct line of distinction between the work, on the one hand and education and past time, on the other. As a result, it never hampered their overall growth and development. But in the era of industrialisation when most of the artisan and household sector gradually disappeared, children of the poorer families started being engaged as labour in the agriculture, and industry segments, mostly belonging to the unorganised sector. Thus exploitation, started creeping in with the change in the nature of work done by the working children. Over the years, it has reached obnoxious proportions in our country.

Child labour also exists in developed countries, such as USA, Italy, Portugal and Spain. However, developing countries can not afford to take trade measures against them. According to ILO estimates, approximately 250 to 300 million children work around the world. Of these the largest concentration is between 5 to 14 year old, and are located in Asia (61 per cent), Africa (32 per cent), Latin America (7 per cent).

Causes of Child Labour

Many a reason can be attributed to the growing menace of child labour in India. Amongst others, the main reasons are poverty, and illiteracy, inequitable distribution of assets, insufficient legislative protection and absence of strong child labour unions.

Poverty

In India, poverty is a major contributing factor which has given rise to the problem of child labour. On an average, 30 per cent of Indian population live below the poverty line. The situation is far more worse in the states of Orissa and Bihar where roughly half of the population live below the poverty line followed by UP, Maharashtra and Andhra Pradesh. Large number of families suffering from the malady of poverty are forced to involve their children as labourers out of desperation and in order to supplement the family income.

Child labour is directly related to high rate of dropouts from the school. The high rate of dropouts is invariably a consequence of poverty. The second reason is that in most places schools are situated in very remote areas and are inaccessible to a sizeable population. The schools also present a stale and dismal picture and hold little attraction for children. Due to lack of funds, many schools do not run regularly with teachers absenting most of the time. Schooling of the children become burdensome for the poor families which involves certain expenses, on one hand and deprives them of the income that accrues from child labour, on the other.

Illiteracy

India is ranked the lowest in the world as far as literacy is concerned. The average rate of literacy according to 1991 census was 52.11 per cent. Some states like Andhra Pradesh, Bihar, Madhya Pradesh, etc., register less than forty per cent literate population. The higher rate of illiteracy prevalent among the population contribute the ignorance of the persons in realising their duties as guardians. So they push their children to join as child labour instead of providing them education and other facilities.

Insufficient Protective Legislations

The practice of engaging child labour is an indicator of the backwardness and inadequacies of rules and regulative measures in India. The country has provisions for almost all the industries which engage children as labour, specifying their working hours, terms and conditions of work, education, wages, etc. But very few units have so far strictly adhered to these rules and the administrative machinery has a callous attitude to enforce the same on the employers of the child labour. Thus, there is hardly any organisational or institutional set up which can protect the children from the miseries of work.

Inequitable Distribution of Land Assets

In India, merely 10 per cent of the privileged class hold 90 per cent of the agricultural land. The rest of the farmers are actually farm labourers who work for wages. Inspite of more than four decades of enforcement of tenancy laws, there has been practically no reform on this front. Even today, most of the tenant farmers are mortgaged to big land holders and rich farmers. Thus the slogan "land to the tiller" has borne little fruit. Most of the poor families on account of insufficient earnings, compel their children to take up jobs in order to supplement their meagre family income.

Lack of Unions

In some industries like bidi, glass, match box, carpet,

bangle, fireworks, etc. children as workers are increasingly preferred. The most plausible reason for their preferential employment in such industries is lack of organisational support to child labour. The working children are usually not associated with any trade union. As such, they have no voice and strength to fight for their dues, rights and privileges. There is no institutional set up which can apprise them of their rights and mandatory provisions. In the absence of proper guidance and patronage, the child labour yields to deprivation and callousness.

In a nutshell, socio-economic conditions will continue to influence greatly the fate of children, contributing to greater incidence of child labour. For the sake of the future of all children, it is highly essential to ensure sustainable economic growth and development especially in countries where incidences of child labour are on the rise.

Legislative Provisions

Protection of rights of child is not a new concept or phenomenon in India. It grew out of a conviction and conscious awareness by the farmers of constitution. As part of Directive Principles of State Policy, Article 34 of the Indian Constitution stipulated that the state shall in particular direct its policy so that 'the health and strength of workers, men and women, and the tender age of children are not abused and that citizens are not forced by economic necessity to enter avocations unsuited to their age or strength'.

The second clause of the Article directs the state to ensure that 'the children are given opportunities and facilities to develop in a healthy manner and in conditions of freedom and dignity and that childhood and youth are protected against exploitation and against moral and material abandonment'.

Articles 24 states that no child below that age of 14 years will be engaged in any factory or mines or any hazardous employment. It says nothing about the elimination of child labour.

A National Policy for Children was declared on August 22, 1974. The National Policy reiterated that 'the State shall take steps to provide free and compulsory education for all children upto the age of 14 for which a time bound programme will be brawn up consistent with the availability of resources'. An important component of the policy is that 'children should be protected against neglect, cruelty and exploitation and that no child under 14 years shall be permitted to be engaged in any hazardous occupation or be made to undertake heavy work'.

Child Labour Prohibition and Regulation Act 1986 has made provisions only for regulating working hours for children, restriction of employment during the night, prohibition of overtime work, etc. Article (45) makes provisions for free and compulsory education to all children upto the age of fourteen years.

Despite the enactment of all such legal provisions, prohibition of child participation in jobs in our country is still elusive. Even after more than five decades of independence, nearly fifty per cent of the children in age group of 6-14 (90 million out of a total of 179 million) are out of school. This is a sad reflection of our polity.

Child Labour: A Ticklish Issue

As long as child labour continues, it is profitable for the poor to have more children; each child starting to earn as early as at the age of five. And each such poor parent is tempted to have supplementary income in the form of wages earned. Most often, than not, for such parents, children are considered as capital which involves a very less investment and cost. Thus, the human mortal at its tender age is used more as a capital or as a commodity than as a human being.

Should children be totally discouraged from working? The answer is not that simple as it seems to be. In developing countries like India, children work not because they have noting better to do, but because extreme poverty forces them to work for a living. Everybody agrees that instead of working in carpet factories, they should be doing better things like going to school, playing games, reading books and eating healthy food. But if there are no proper schools, and there are no teachers, no proper social security network, conditions of penury drive them to menial work. Out of the several economic and social reasons for which children are put on jobs, the most obvious reason is poverty of parents which compels them to send their children to jobs than to school. Even where schooling is free, children are still sent to work as without their income, parents and other members of the family become even poorer. So, if people are seriously worried about working children, they should do something to alleviate poverty. Curbing trade curbs incomes, and actually increases poverty. So trade restrictions may actually prove counter productive and ultimately work against the welfare of the working children.

If there be no proper growth of children of today, the future of the country will be in dark. Admittedly, it is the obligation of every generation to properly bring up children who are the citizens of tomorrow. Today's children will be leaders of tomorrow who will hold aloft the banner of the nation. If a child fails to receive proper attention, training and guidance, it will indeed be a blot of the society and of the government of the day. Every society, therefore, must devote full attention to ensure that children are properly cared for and brought up in an appropriate atmosphere where they could receive adequate training, education and guidance so that they are able to occupy their rightful place in the society when they grow up.

Child labour is necessarily the outcome of the social circumstances and economic conditions existing in our country. It is a practice undertaken by the children to provide economic support to their families in the short run. Also it is a social evil as much as it impairs the mental and physical development of children in the long run.

The issue of child labour can be viewed from the supply side and the demand side. On the demand side, the 'nimble fingers' of the children are very much sought after. Child labour is a cheap and therefore quite economical for the employer. And there are umpteen non-economic advantages in employing them.

On the supply side, pressure of population, acute poverty of the people, existence of unorganised sector and urbanisation are some of the causes leading to the incidence of child labour. In the ultimate analysis child labour creates more adverse effects than beneficial ones for a developing society like India. The children are deprived of education. Their health is affected, normal family life is jeopardised and the social control is lost. The child labour compete with adult labourers and ultimately falls victim of depressed wages. These children, deprived of the precious memories of childhood, grow up into ignorant adults with hardly any type of intellectual gain.

A close examination of the problem indicates that if child labour is totally eliminated in India, thousands of families will be affected. Whether admitted or not it is hardly possible to eliminate child labour in India under the prevailing socio-economic condition. Therefore, instead of eliminating it, child labour can be protected from both physical and mental exploitation. Introducing time wage system, suitable safety measures in the factory, a fair amount of compensation for accidents and keeping the children from hazardous occupations are some of the reforms, which should be undertaken.

Few will disagree, that a child labour is better placed than a street urchin, a vagabond; at least, he does not indulge in anti-social activities. So, in the interest of child labour in particular and of the nation in general, steps should be taken to save child labour from exploitation like working in hazardous conditions, long hours of work, meagre wages, physical assault, lack of basic amenities at the workplace, etc.

A boy who works as a 'coolie' or assistant to a senior mason today masters the skill and becomes himself a mason tomorrow and the builders would flock to him for construction work. The coolie of today becomes a petty contractor tomorrow with a band of workers working under him. Similar is the case with an auto-mechanic assistant. Tomorrow, babus with 2-wheelers and four wheelers will be standing in queue in front of his garage to have their vehicles repaired. No doubt, the child worker at the initial stages is exploited, still he manages to establish himself professionally and financially in the long run.

Epilogue

Government agencies and NGOs need to come forward to establish training institutes imparting vocational education on the lines of ITI and polytechnic schools for masonry, carpentry and auto-repair work, etc. alongwith formal education. While doing so it should also be borne in mind that a child labour in a majority of cases works for his livelihood and not just for fun. Therefore eradication of child labour totally at one go is hardly possible and desirable.

In a developing country like India the status given to child labour and the role assigned to them is far from satisfactory. They are discriminated, humiliated and harassed and are not treated at par with their adult counterparts in several spheres of activities. The problem of child labour at workplace is uncountable. They are blamed, tortured and harassed by their boss. They need cooperation, sympathy and helpful approach from all concerned if they are to convert their weaknesses into strength.

References

1. *Economic Times, 23rd* August, 1996.
2. *Main Stream*, p. 129, 18th Nov., 1995.
3. *Economic Times*, 16th June, 1999.
4. *Yojana*, January, 1996.
5. *Southern Economist*, June, 1999.
6. *Yojana*, July 1997.
7. *Mainstream*, 23rd August, 1997.
8. *Southern Economist*, May 1, 1994.
9. *Rights of the Child, UNICEF* India Country Office, 1991.
10. *Yojana*, January, 1996.

2

Role of the National Child Labour Project in Berhampur City of Orissa

*Pitambar Dash

Introduction

A growing focus on the elimination of child labour in the country has led the Ministry of Labour, Government of India to execute several plans and programmes and the National Child Labour Project (NCLP) is one of the major programmes implemented throughout the country. In Orissa 16 NCLPs are operating since December 1995 in 16 districts where the concentration of child labour is apparently high. One such project is working in Ganjam district.

The present work aims at analysing the working of the National Child Labour Project (NCLP) in the City of Berhampur. Prior to the direction made by the Hon'ble

---

* Dr. Pitambar Dash is a Reader (Senior) in Economics in Govt. Science College, Chatrapur (Orissa). The present work is a part of the findings of the U.G.C. (Minor) Research project conducted by Dr. Dash.

Supreme Court of India, the National Child Labour Project had taken up survey for identification and detection of child labour within the Municipal area of Berhampur, Ganjam. The National Child Labour Project (NCLP) Society for Welfare of Child Labour, Berhampur (Ganjam) Orissa was registered under the Societies Registration Act vide Regd. No. GJM–3944/95–96.

As per the guidelines, the Collector, Ganjam is the President of the Society for Welfare Child Labour, Berhampur under the National Child Labour Project and Asst. Labour Commissioner Berhampur is the Working-President, District Labour Officer, Asst. Labour Officer, Berhampur, Assistant Labour Officer, Chatrapur, Rural Labour Inspector Berhampur, Chatrapur are the executive members of the Society. Where as the Collector, Ganjam is continuing to function as the Chairman of the National Child Labour Project, Berhampur. The National Child Labour Project is headed by the Project Director, having its office at Berhampur and assisted by two qualified Field Officers to carry out day-to-day activities of the Project. The National Child Labour Project at Berhampur has started 15 Special Schools (SS) in different child labour prone areas of Berhampur Municipality. In each school three Educational Instructors are imparting education to the children. The task of the instructors is to motivate the parents and to bring the children to the school for education. Non-traditional and vocational education is imparted to the children of these schools. The students are given free education and the study materials. The school uniform is maintained to give an insignia of the students of NCLP. The students are provided free nutrition and mid-day meals in each school. Since all the children are drawn out from a vocation or other, there is a provision for giving stipend to each such child at the rate of Rs. 100/- per month which is deposited in the name of the children but they being minor, the pass book is operated jointly by the Project Director and guardians.

The periodical health check-ups is conducted in every school by I.C.D.S. Medical Officer, Urban Health Centre and NGOs. In acute cases, the children are referred to M.K.C.G. Medical College and Hospital, Berhampur under the assistance of District Red Cross Society. The Project Director and Field Officer are almost mobile to take care of the proper functioning of the schools and regular teaching by teachers.

In order to generate interest among the parents, teachers and also the students, different functions are conducted and competitions are made with prize giving ceremony from time to time.

In order to generate mass awareness about the employment and exploitation of child labour, mass media programme are being organised through pamphlets and television programmes. Besides, a documentary film on child labour under the name and style of *'Samikhya'* is telecast in regional programme of Doordarshan. The employment and exploitation of child labour was organised by way of street play known as *'Surya Sikha'*. Moreover *'Loka Nrutya'* through the medium of *'Dasakathia'* is displayed. To discourage the employment of child labour, the NCPL participates in the global march against child labour organised within the Municipal area of Berhampur town. Seminars and symposia are being conducted from time to time to discourage the employment of child labour and for universalisation of primary education.

Location of Special Schools

Out of 20 special schools in Ganjam district, 15 schools are opened in Berhampur Municipal area. One more special school is going to be opened at Khodasingi area of Berhampur to impart non-traditional education and vocational training to 50 girl child labourers of the locality. The schools are located in slum pockets as well as developed areas of the city. From the year 1999–2000, the special schools (SS) are being adopted by the reputed NGOs of the city. The details of the location of SS and NGOs adopted them are given below:

Table—2.1 The Location of Special Schools and NGO's

Sl. No.	*Name of SS*	*Adopted by NGOs*
1.	Gate Bazar	GEOSEA
2.	Aska Road–I	GRAM JYOTI
3.	Aska Road–II	AWAKE
4.	Corporation Road (Khaha Street)	GEOSEA
5.	Haridakhandi	GRAM JYOTI
6.	Aska Road 1st Gate	AWAKE
7.	Bijipur	JEEVAN DHARA
8.	Gosaninugam–I	ISRD
9.	NH-5 Ankoli	JEEVAN DHARA
10.	Gandhi Nagar	ISRD
11.	Goilundi	GEOSEA
12.	Ankoli	SWE
13.	Jaleswar Khandi	SWE
14.	Puruna Berhampur	SMILE
15.	Gosaninuagam–II	ISRD

Amount of Grant Received from Government

The NCLP of Berhampur has received grants as per the details given below:

Table—2.2 Amount of Grant Received (1995–2001)

Year	*Amount received*	*Amount spent*
1995-96	Rs. 15,27,100	Rs. 2,95,113
1996-97	Rs. 40,37,342	Rs. 27,73,755
1997-98	Rs. 20,62,650	Rs. 36,37,880
1998-99	Rs. 47,95,375	Rs. 38,74,142
N.A.	—	—
2000-02	Rs. 44,75,819	Rs. 9,83,508

Source: *Annual Reports of the NCLP, Berhampur.*

The NCLP of Berhampur received grant in a number of installments from the Government. The heads of expenditure are ear-marked by the Government and hence the total amount of grant received varies from year to year.

Type of Informal Education Imparted in Special Schools

The entire course content of the formal schools is divided in to three parts and it is completed in three years only. In the first year the course of Class–I and II is covered the second year covers the courses of Class–III and IV and in the third year the course of Class–V of the formal school is covered.

Vocational Training

The children are given of the vocational training in trades like tailoring, textile, toy making, coir mats making, coconut shell craft, rubber stamp making, mushroom culture, embroidery works, solo craft, printing, wool knitting, bamboo crafts, plywood works, appliqué making etc. Vocational training is imparted from 1 pm. to 5 pm. SAHARA, a leading

NGO of Berhampur has been entrusted with the task of providing vocational education to such children. The NGO is paid Rs. 5/- per child per month and at about Rs. 90,000/- per year from the NCLP, Berhampur towards its remuneration.

Infrastructure of the Special Schools

The special schools are functioning in private rented houses with a monthly rent of Rs. 1,000/-. The houses are very small in size, dark and unventilated. The toilet facilities is unsuitable and inadequate for a large number of boys and girls of such schools. There is dearth of drinking water in such schools.

There is a provision for 3 teachers and 2 vocational teachers and a clerk and a peon for a school with 100 children. Employees, due to uncertainty, lack of sense of commitment and involvement in welfare works of children. It is reported that by the end of 2001, March, 31, about 2000 children have been enrolled and by the end of the last year of second term (by the end of 2002) all the child labourers identified in the survey of 1996 will be covered.

Food and Nutrition

In addition to rice and dal provided through the mid-day meal programme, the NCLP of Berhampur provides nutritious food worth Rs. 2.50/- per student per day. In the mid day there is provision for supplying bread and egg to such children. Hence both the children and the parents designate such schools as *"Anda and Ruti Schools"*.

Evaluation of the NCLP of Berhampur

1. The NCLP of Berhampur identifies only 2905 child labourers engaged in various hazardous and non-hazardous occupations in its door to door survey conducted in 1996. The actual number of child

labourers exceeds 5237. The NCLP, during its survey could not identify a single child labourer engaged in any hazardous occupation. In fact, 628 child labourers are actually engaged in hazardous occupations as defined in the child labour Act of 1986.

2. The quality of informal education imparted to such students is very poor. Test results reveal that the children of formal schools are a better in ability to grasp the subject and working out sums. Hence, the children of non formal schools have failed to compete with the students of formal schools.

3. It is found that only 30 per cent of child labourers are admitted to such schools and the rest of the children are transferred from other schools where no such benefits are available.

4. These schools are located in private rented houses which are very small unventilated and dark. The children sit on the floor. Even the teachers are not provided with furniture for use.

5. The children of special schools are given vocational training by a local NGO, SAHARA. The project officer himself admits of the bottlenecks in the supply of raw materials, instruments and implements. The marketing of such products becomes a problem. It can be said that different types of trades that are taught to them cannot help these children in earning a livelihood in future.

6. In order to generate awareness about employment and exploitation of child labour, the NCLP has done no visible work till date. Parents, employees and the public in general remain in different about the plight of child labour.

3

Child Labour in India: Problems and Perspectives

*Mr. Pitabas Pradhan
*Dr. Kamalun Nabi

Introduction

Childhood, the most impressionable period of human life, is perhaps the most longed for whims every adult would fancy to relapse into—sweet, carefree moments, unaware of the trauma of life. During this formative period, a child imbibes the basic traits of developing personality, responsibilities, and traits. A happy childhood is the right of every child and providing it is the concern of every nation. Children are the most important asset of the society. The welfare and development of any community depends largely on the health and well being of its children.

* Mr. Pradhan, Research Scholar, Department of Industrial Relations and Personnel Management, Berhampur University—760 007, Orissa.
* Dr. Nabi. Lecturer in Commerce, R.C.M. Science College, Khallikote, 761 030, Orissa.

The good physical and mental health of a nation and the advancement of a civilization demands the fulfillment of the obligation to the younger generation by opening up all vistas of opportunities for every child to unfold its personality and rise to its full stature-physical, moral, mental and spiritual.

Barring the fundamental societal rights for survival and the provisions of the state for proper health care, nutrition, and environment, children as an important segment of the society, need protection from discrimination, exploitation and abuse. Similarly, the rights of development through proper education, care, social security, leisure, recreation and cultural activities are the basic tenets on which the healthy growth of a nation depends upon. Last but not the least, the rights of participation through freedom of expression, thought, conscience and religion, freedom of association and peaceful harmony, right to information and awareness are some other considerations civilized can hardly bypass.

There have been constant efforts at the national and international level for the protection of these rights. But an observation of the global situation forces one to believe that either our efforts in this direction are inadequate or we have failed to address to the roots of the problem.

Instances of child abuse can be cited through the examples of gender discrimination against the girl child, employment of child labour, child prostitution, child beggary, child destitution in orphanages use of the child in terrorist activities and war etc. It is estimated that there are 17.38 million working children, 5 million street children and 4,00,000 child prostitutes in India. However, the major form of child abuse, a chief concern for the entire human civilization, is the forced employment of children as child labourers.

Concept of Child Labour

Child Labour can be denominated to all those acts of employment of children of less than a specified legal age. A 'child' is some one who needs adult protection for physical, psychological and intellectual development until able to become independently integrated into adult world. Most of the labour laws in India interpret 'child' as any person below 14 years. 'Labour', on the other hand, refers to any work, whether manual or mental, which is also synonymous with 'Wage Labour', denotes to the workers who do not have any other adequate source of livelihood except the sale of their labour power, i.e. capacity to work either physically or mentally, in return of which they get wage/salary. Thus labour includes workers of both head and hand, who work for others for a given payment in cash/kind. Thus child labour includes all those persons who have not completed 14 years of age and work for others for remuneration.

The Problem of Child Labour in India

According to the report of the ILO, as many as 250 million children from the ages 10 to 14 work in jobs are perilous by nature, out of which 55 million are in India alone.

The number of child labourers in formal sector in 1991 stood at 1.12 crore. Out of the total child population of 24.21 crores about one-third were potential child workers. According to the UNESCO Report 2000, nearly six per cent of children that constitutes over 1.39 crore children in the age groups of 5 to 14 in India work as labourers in various formal sectors. The figure however excludes those working in informal sectors or those who are engaged for domestic chores. The most stunning about it is that the number of child labourers registered an increase of 27.19 lakh during the past decade. According to the study Andhra Pradesh had 23.64 lakh working children which was the highest in the country followed by Uttar Pradesh with 19.20 lakh, Rajasthan with 15.64 lakh and Bihar with 8.36 lakh child labourers.

The practice of child labour in one form or other is very old in India and is extant since time immemorial. Child labourers are exploited, exposed to hazardous work condition and paid a pittance for their long hours of work. Forced to forego education, and shoulder the filial responsibilities, they bear the social brunt at an age when their peers have yet to leave the cocoons of parental protection. These children never know what childhood is. To earn their livelihood, they are forced to work in hazardous occupations like the glass, match, fireworks, and tobacco industries. Most of the deprived lot, eke out a living as domestic servants or helpers at tea stalls or at construction sites. Thus unfortunately, children who should be the most protected are undeniably the most vulnerable to greater deprivation and neglect.

It is therefore ominous for India that the number of child labourers is on the rise despite of an increase in social consciousness and enactment of several prohibitory laws.

Constitutional Provisions

The constitution of India under various provisions contained in Part–III and IV, provides for prevention of child labourers:

Article 15 (3) empowers the state to make any special provisions for the welfare of women and children.

Article 23 prohibits the traffic in human beings and forced labour in all its forms.

Article 24 prohibits employment of children below the age of 14 years in hazardous jobs.

Article 37 (e) makes it duty of the state to prevent the children from entering into jobs unsuited to their ages.

Article 39 (f) recommends for the protection of childhood against exploitation and moral and material abandonment.

Article-45 directs the state to provide free and compulsory education to all children upto 14 years of age with in 10 years of adopting the constitution.

Legal Enactments Prohibiting Employment of Child Labour

Besides the constitutional safeguards, different labour enactments also contain provisions which aims at prevention and in some cases regulation of the employment of children. The various laws enacted are:

The factories Act, 1948, prohibits the employment of children below 15 years of age.

The Motor Transport Workers Act, 1961 prohibits the employment of children below 15 years of age in motor transport undertakings.

The Bidi and Cigar Workers (Condition of Employment) Act, 1966 prohibits employment of children below the age of 14 years in any industrial premises. The employment of adolescent between the age group of 14 to 18 years is prohibited between 7 p.m. to 6 a.m.

The Apprentices Act, 1961 prohibits persons below 14 years to join as apprentices training except in the case of vocational training.

The various provision under the above discussed labour laws have failed to serve the purpose, perhaps due to the feeling that these labour laws do not provide any deterrent punishment. But with a firm commitment to provide better safeguards to child workers, the Government of India in 1986, enacted the Child Labour (Prohibition and Regulation) Act, 1986 for prohibiting and regulating the employment of child labour.

The Act aimed to fulfill the following objectives:

- To bring uniformity in the definition of child in the related labour laws and defined child as any person who has not completed his 14 years of age.

- To ban employment of children in certain occupations and processes considered to be hazardous.
- To enable the government modify the scope of banned industries and process by laying down a procedure.
- To regulate conditions of work of children when it is not possible to prohibit them from working.
- To lay deterrent punishment for violation of the provisions of law on child labour.

In fact, the act forbids the employment of children below 14 years. It was expected that by making the laws more stringent, the national goal of prohibition and regulation of child labour could be realized.

Moving a step ahead, the Supreme Court in a significant judgment in December 1996 banned child labour and held employers responsible for the rehabilitation of the children employed by them. In a bid to check exploitation of child labour in hazardous industries, the court directed that all offending employers must pay compensation of Rs. 20,000 for every child and the state was to pay Rs. 5,000 towards the rehabilitation of each child labour rescued. Income generated from this corpus would be used to ensure the child's education in suitable institution.

The Government of India, in September 1994 constituted a National Authority for eliminating child labour. An ambitious Rs. 850 crore scheme was launched to eliminate child labour in manufacturing and service sectors over a period of five years, which became operational in eleven states in April 1995.

In addition, Article 32 of the United Nations convention on the rights of the child 1989, which the Government of India has also ratified, lays down that state parties recognize the rights of the child to protection from economic exploitation and from performing any work that is likely to be hazardous or to interfere with the child's education, or to be harmful to the child's health or physical, mental, spiritual, moral and social development.

In spite of all these Acts, the problem of child labour is a persisting one. The irony is that in spite of all our efforts we have achieved very little success in the child labour front. The proportion of child labourers rescued is negligible. The higher ups in the labour department agree that it is difficult to eliminate child labour, though it can only be regulated. Participating in a 5 day seminar on Child Labour jointly organised by the V.V. Giri National Labour Institute and Orissa state Labour Institute, the commissioner admitted that "Child labour is in the net of poverty, illiteracy and other social factors, which is difficult to eliminate".

Causes of Child Labour

The main causes of employment of child labour in India, as identified by many studies are:

(i) Poverty, *(ii)* Illiteracy, *(iii)* Inadequate legislative measures, *(iv)* Willingness of people to employ child labour for profit, *(v)* Lack of enforcement of legislation, *(vi)* Population explosion, *(vii)* Inadequate health care facilities in the rural areas, *(viii)* Inappropriate policy and poor educational infrastructure in the villages, *(ix)* Resource constraints, *(x)* Lack of awareness (community consciousness).

The UNICEF in its 1997 State of the World's Children Report, proposed six key steps that must be taken to address the problem. Immediate elimination of hazardous child labour, free and compulsory education for all children, stringent anti-child labour laws and their vigorous enforcement, registration of all children at birth, data collection and monitoring of child labour and code of conduct and procurement policies were the key suggestions of the Report.

Though poverty is the root cause of employment of child labour in India, the UNICEF very appropriately, has challenged the myth that child labour can never be eliminated until poverty disappears. In fact, child labour exists because there are people willing to use children for profit—to exploit their poverty, but not because India is a poor country. While the efforts to eliminate all forms of child labour must go hand in hand with measures to reduce extreme poverty, the end of hazardous child labour must not wait for the end of poverty.

The most important requirement in the drive against child labour is free and compulsory education for all children up to 14 years of age. Enforcement of the relevant constitutional provision with commitment will without any doubt solve more than 50 per cent of the problem.

The Muniram Saikia Committee has pointed out that, in India more than 6 crore 40 lakh children in the age group of 6 to 14 years are deprived from school education, out of which 3 crore are in 6-10 age group and the remaining 3.4 crores are in the 11-14 age group. The UNESCO report said "there is significant positive correlation between out of school children and proportion of child labourers."

The commission on labour standards, headed by Subramaniam Swamy, had estimated that abolition of child labour in the country by 2004 would cost Rs. 15,000 crores, which the government can mobilize by reducing wasteful expenditure.

However, the most important support will come from the individual through their awareness and their insistence that the rights of the child be respected. The mass media should take the responsibility of creating awareness among the public on protection of the rights of the children and against their employment as labourers. Therefore, the need of the hour is to create world wide consciousness in order to change the attitude of the society towards children. In a country like India, the mass media has the credibility before the public because of the societal and constitutional protection it enjoys. This can be a major asset in our effort to eradicate child labour.

The media's intervention for advocacy and awareness can comprise the following steps:

- Sensitizing administrators.
- Reminding the government of the commitments made.
- Informing people of the existing legal provisions.
- Educating parents.
- Bridging information and awareness gaps.
- Monitoring and protecting the employment of children.
- Making children understand their rights.
- Promoting democratic process of participatory development.

The general tendency in the modern development of child labour has been the strengthening of the statutory requirements and collective efforts at the expense of rights and obligations created by the state and its individuals. How important these latter remain depends, of course, on the vicissitude of the problem in the given society as well as the efficacy of the law enforcing agencies and the socially responsible groups allowed by the actual operation of the economy.

References

1. Malik P.L., *Industrial Law*, Vol. 1 and 2, Eastern Book Company, Lucknow, 1992.

2. Bhogliwala, T.N., *Economics of Labour and Industrial Relations*, Sahitya Bhawan Publications, Agra, 1996.

3. Goswami, V.G., *Labour and Industrial Law*, Central Law Agency, Allahabad, 1993.

4. Punhani R., "Rights of the Child—Role of the Media", *Social Welfare*, December 1995.

5. *VVGNLI News Letter*, June-July, 1996.

4

Child Labour in Transport Sector—A Study

***Dr. R.N. Misra**
****Santosh Kumar Pradhan**

The term labour is used in various sectors. Labour includes work for others for a given remuneration of cash and kind. Labour is considered as a manpower resource. It is a primary factor in the field of production.

Now-a-days child labour forms almost every section of the community and has now become a front page news. In the cities, towns and villages of the present civilization of the world we can see countless little children at work, earning their livelihood for supporting their parents with as much responsibility with competition as to adult labourers. A child labour has practically no choice but to work in order to get rid of hunger and starvation. Child labour is a person who come in the age group of 7 to 14 years as per the labour Act, 1948.

* Dr. R.N. Misra, Senior Faculty Member of Deptt. of Commerce. Science College, Hinjilicut.

** Mr. Santosh Kumar Pradhan, Research Scholar.

When the business of wage earning or participation in self or family support conflicts directly with the business of growth and education, the result is child labour. Poverty, liabilities, landlessness, lack of educational facilities, orphanage, financial burden upon the families etc. are the main factors which force the child to work for assisting their poor parents. In rural areas more then 82 per cent of total child labour force work in agricultural and rest in fisheries, cottage industries and small retail business. But in urban areas child labour is found almost in every sector starting from household to transportation.

The history of child labour legislation in India is related to the history of exploitation of child labour as work for the child who moved out from the home and the village field to work in hazardous occupation. The various stages in which the child has received protection in India are as follows from Factories Act 1881 upto Child Labour (Prohibition and Regulation) Act 1986. The Act prohibits children from the working in either hazardous or non-hazardous activities. But in practice the fact is that children are devoting their time and energy almost in every sector. Today they are found working in public office like medical, Police Station etc.

The Results of Child Labour Survey in Orissa—1997

Table—4.1 clearly shows that in every district of the Orissa State, large number of children engaged both in the hazardous and non-hazardous occupation. Nabarangpur district has the highest child-labour whereas Jagatsinghpur has the lowest.

In this paper we have made an attempt to study about the child labour engaged in the transport sector only. Lack of sufficient time and resources we have chosen only Aska town of Ganjam District for the purpose.

Coming to the historic town of Aska, its origin can be traced back to the dates of Kalinga War. The word *'Asika'* is

Table—4.1 Results of Child Labour Survey in Orissa–1997

Sl. No.	Name of the District	No. of Establishment/work sites covered in the survey			No. of Establishments/work sites found to be engaged child labour		
		Hazard	Non Hazard	Total	Hazard	Non Hazard	Total
1	**2**	**3**	**4**	**5**	**6**	**7**	**8**
1.	Nayagarh	251	7789	8040	137	2109	2246
2.	Bargarh	79	1917	1996	67	1816	1883
3.	Boudh	88	984	1072	25	621	646
4.	Khurda	373	5736	6109	55	488	543
5.	Balasore	628	12260	12888	376	10453	10829
6.	Rayagada	9	12963	12972	2	11968	11970
7.	Sambalpur	377	1240	1617	324	727	1051
8.	Jajpur	28	1963	1991	19	1938	1957
9.	Bhadrak	158	10664	10822	1	4924	4925
10.	Malkangiri	1620	7124	8744	1519	7080	8599
11.	Angul	629	2543	3172	294	166	460
12.	Kandhamal	0	6456	6456	0	5692	5692
13.	Ganjam	1046	5307	6353	848	781	1629

(Contd...)

Table—4.1 (Contd...)

1	2	3	4	5	6	7	8
14.	Kalahandi	53	15481	15534	0	14073	14073
15.	Sundergarh	243	3494	3737	7	459	466
16.	Nebarangpur	1027	23961	24988	1026	23961	24987
17.	Koraput	2351	14597	16948	21	12620	12641
18.	Jharsuguda	1390	5294	6684	993	3888	4881
19.	Dhenkanal	698	5406	6104	13	1739	1752
20.	Jagatsinghpur	2	404	406	2	278	280
21.	Gajapati	2034	10315	12349	1865	7562	9427
22.	Nuapada	1223	6412	7635	873	1181	2054
23.	Cuttack	1554	5781	7335	1197	5221	6418
24.	Mayurbhanja	3627	27146	30773	811	16498	17309
25.	Bolangir	1515	9988	11503	1515	9988	11503
26.	Deogarh	37	3990	4027	37	3954	3991
27.	Sonepur	819	2936	3755	819	1543	2362
28.	Puri	159	8405	8564	13	781	794
29.	Kendrapara	153	5920	6073	153	5915	6068
30.	Keonjhar	372	5692	6064	71	3304	3375
	Total	**22543**	**232168**	**254711**	**13083**	**161728**	**174811**

(Contd...)

Table—4.1 (Contd...)

Sl. No.	Name of the District	Total Child Labour Identified								
		Hazardous			Non Hazardous			Grand Total		
		Male	Female	Total	Male	Female	Total	Male	Female	Total
1	2	3	4	5	6	7	8	9	10	11
1.	Nayagarh	72	65	137	1692	417	2109	1764	482	2246
2.	Bargarh	70	39	109	1338	641	1979	1408	680	2088
3.	Boudh	10	19	29	3601	2770	6371	3611	2789	6400
4.	Khurda	35	34	69	1221	576	1797	1256	610	1866
5.	Balasore	271	166	437	6276	5306	11582	6547	5472	12019
6.	Rayagada	2	0	2	7455	4785	12240	7457	4785	12242
7.	Sambalpur	1248	3563	4811	487	341	828	1735	3904	5639
8.	Jajpur	22	15	37	1550	470	2020	1572	485	2057
9.	Bhadrak	8	2	10	3364	2023	5387	3372	2025	5397
10.	Malkangiri	1074	999	2073	5236	2981	8217	6310	3980	10290
11.	Angul	991	1784	2775	178	74	252	1169	1858	3027
12.	Kandhamal	0	0	0	3376	3080	6456	3376	3080	6456
13.	Ganjam	296	564	860	700	312	1012	996	876	1872

(Contd...)

Table—4.1 (Contd...)

1	2	3	4	5	6	7	8	9	10	11
14.	Kalahandi	0	0	0	8613	6097	14710	8613	6097	14710
15.	Sundergarh	16	47	63	634	174	808	650	221	871
16.	Nebarangpur	635	532	1167	17963	13554	31517	18598	14086	32684
17.	Koraput	78	156	234	7040	6284	13324	7118	6440	13558
18.	Jharsuguda	560	1255	1815	2250	2619	4869	2810	3874	6684
19.	Dhenkanal	24	9	33	1183	686	1869	1207	695	1902
20.	Jagatsinghpur	3	5	8	281	123	404	284	128	412
21.	Gajapati	905	1123	2028	4330	3867	8197	5235	4990	10225
22.	Nuapada	737	260	997	1106	114	1220	1843	374	2217
23.	Cuttack	726	805	1531	3772	2124	5896	4498	2929	7427
24.	Mayurbhanja	602	472	1074	11072	9609	20681	11674	10081	21755
25.	Bolangir	972	732	1704	6403	4168	10571	7375	4900	12275
26.	Deogarh	156	269	428	2185	2297	4482	2344	2566	4910
27.	Sonepur	621	394	1015	1293	329	1622	1914	723	2637
28.	Puri	15	10	25	730	182	912	745	192	937
29.	Kendrapara	76	101	177	4130	1932	6062	4206	2033	6239
30.	Keonjhar	66	47	113	1773	2294	4067	1839	2341	4180
	Total	**10294**	**13467**	**23761**	**111232**	**80229**	**191461**	**121526**	**93696**	**215222**

said to be derived from the word *'Asoka'* the branded name of Emperor Asoka of Magadha who killed and injured fighter people of Kalinga in the terrible Kalinga War of 261 B.C. which took place on the bank of River Daya near Dhauli mountain. Some Prisoners of War after being released came and settled on the northern bank of river Rushikulya near a Buddhist Vihar and called the village *'Asoka'* which in course of time was known as *Asika.* The British called it Aska.

According to another legend the ill-fated wives of Rushikulya region went to the spot of Kalinga War to see the dead bodies of their husband. They reached the spot and uttered the word *'Rascal Ashoka'*, weeping, abusing scolding and branding the emperor Ashoka who was responsible for the death of their husbands. At this situation some of the Buddhist monks came to their help, gave them courage and accompanied with their return journey to their native place, when they reached their village the Buddhist monks gave the consolation and advised them not to express sorrow from which date the village was known as Aa-soka (not to weep). Asika is the corrupted form of Aa-soka.

Aska is proud of Ganjam district. It is the centre of learning and cultural, trade and commerce. During the British period it was the headquarters of the Sub-Registrar and the district Munsif situated on the Banks of the Bada Nadi and Rushikulya river. This town was mainly famous for the Aska Sugar factory which was the first Sugar Factory of South-East-Asia. The factory was established in 1854 A.D. at Aska on the bank of river Rushikulya by the Pyari Company of the Madras city. Frederic James Vian Minchin who was a retired soldier of German Army was appointed as the Manager of this sugar factory.

The present main building of the Hari Har high school, Aska was his residence. In order to improve the transport facility of the factory as well as the communication of the town. Mr. Minchin demanded before the British authorities for the construction of a bridge over the river Rushikulya at Aska which was completed in 1857. But unfortunately the same was destroyed on 4.11.1990 by the devastating flood of Rushikulya.

Mr. Minchin died in 1903 at Gopalpur-on-sea. Thereafter his wife Sona Minchin managed the factory till her death on 15.11.1916. Consequently the factory was purchased and managed by a rich man namely Paramananda Sahu of village Nimakhandi of Berhampur Estate. Thereafter this factory is shifted to Nuagam in 1964. Aska is proud of the Utkal Ayurvedic Co-op. Pharmacy Ltd. which is a pioneering indigenous machine manufacturing institution of the State. Aska is also famous for its natural beauty by its surrounding Mandir, Masjid, Church, it is a holy place, large number of pilgrims took holy dips at the Sangam place of river Rushikulya and Bada Nadi. It is the forecasting place of National integration.

Aska is situated at the central place of Ganjam District with communication to Metro cities like Bhubaneswar, Cuttack, Berhampur, Rourkella, Durgapur, and Sambalpur. Large number of vehicles are plying in every minute by carrying passengers and goods. To communicate rural areas, small town of the Aska constituency many vehicles like mini buses, trekkers, trax, jeeps, Autos, Cars are plying every day from early in the morning till late midnight.

On this account more than 300 vehicles are plying daily with the help of tiny little masters whose age is below 14 years.

As the centre place of trade of business, learning and culture it communicated rural areas, small and big town of Ganjam District so many vehicles are plying from Aska to other places. They are illustrated in the Table—4.2.

The Table—4.2 clearly shows that large number of vehicles are playing short or long distance from Aska to different place to Ganjam district or outside.

Table—4.2 Type of Transport and Distance of Journey per Day

Sl. No.	*Types of Vehicles*	*No. of Vehicles*	*Distance of journey per day*		
			From	*To*	*Kms.*
1.	Mini buses, 407, 608 Mahindra, Villagers	85	Aska	Berhampur	160
2.	Trakker	35	-do-	Sorada	120
	Trax	45	-do-	Bhanjanagar	160
3.	Car	35	-do-	Buguda	120
4.	Auto	45	-do-	Digapahandi	120
5.	Jeep	35	-do-	Polosara	72
6.	Marshal	20	-do-	K.S. Nagar	72
		—	-do-	Ballipadar	90
		—	-do-	Purusottampur	90
		—	-do-	Ballisira	90
		—	-do-	Jahada	50
		—	-do-	Chatrapur	140

Indeed, large number of child labour are engaged in the transport sector are male children of all castes.

The number of child labour employed in the transport sector accordingly to sex, age, education, class and exhibited in the Table—4.3.

The Table—4.3 shows that the age group of child labour is 7 to 14, children of all castes are employed in this hazardous work with a lower rates of wages per day.

Table—4.3 Details of the Child Labour in the Transport Sector

Age group	Class				Total	Education classes			Wage per day
	SC	ST	OBC	Gen.		I-V	VI-VIII	VIII-IX	Rs.
6–8	6	2	4	4	16	10	6	—	10
8–10	8	3	5	5	21	7	14	—	10
10–12	10	4	4	5	23	9	6	8	15
12–14	9	2	8	7	26	6	14	6	15
Total	**33**	**11**	**21**	**21**	**86**				

Source : Collected from direct personal interview with informants.

All of them are literates (how to write and read.) Due to lack of adequate income of parents they had to come forward in search of employment at joined in this hazardous sector. They have no bargaining power, they work as per the desire of the owner with, "No work no pay" condition. They are employed on temporary basis.

The working hours of these tiny masters are not fixed, they resume their work early in the morning and relieve till the end of the journey which may be midnight. They work as a cleaner, money collector and a guider of the vehicles.

They also work in the repair section of the vehicles. In every garage, child labour works as a little mechanic master. Their total strength in different garage, presented in Table—4.4.

The Table—4.4 shows that children of all caste groups are engaged in these garages. They work long hours of day as that of adult labourers.

Table—4.4 Child Labour Strength in Repairs Section of Various Motor Garage of Aska Town

Sl. No.	Name of garage	Age group of child labour	Category to children				Per day hour of working
			SC	ST	OBC	Gen.	
1.	Ashok motor garage (Two wheeler)	10–12 12–14	2	—	2	3	10 hrs.
2.	Mahima motor garage	10–12 12–14	3	1	4	5	10 hrs.
3.	Bhanjanagar motor garage (Four wheeler)	12–14 14–16	4	2	6	4	10 hrs.
4.	Gundicha motor garage (Two wheeler)	12–14 14–16	5	3	8	4	10 hrs.
5.	Maharana motor garage (Two wheeler)	12–14 14–16	3	2	7	5	10 hrs.
		Total	**17**	**8**	**27**	**21**	

Source : Collected for direct personal interview with informants.

As they work in this hazardous occupation but the benefits granted by the owner is a dream for them. There is no economical and social helps granted by the owner to them as per the Government rules. If there is an accident faced by the child labour during the work period, they may seriously injured but no one takes care of them, including the owner. The owner, however receives the insurance claim to compensate the loss of the vehicles. He agrees to help the child labour through wage reduction agreement or as media of work or reimbursement of expenses. Social security benefit like payment of bonus, gratuity, P.F. workmen's compensation are dreams for them.

Economic Backwardness is one of the main reasons that forces parents to send their children to work, but exploitative child labour practice is a deliberate action on the part of employer for profit motive. The most significant cause of the employment of children is widespread poverty. According to an estimate if all children are eliminated from the work force, in India, there will be additional employment opportunities for at least 15 million adult unemployed persons.

In the report of labour statistics in Orissa 2000, following were seminars and workshops organised by the Labour Directorate and State Labour Institutes for the prohibition of child labour in the hazardous occupations in different district levels are:

1. The State labour institute organised Zonal level training-cum-workshops on the enforcement of child labour act in the Indal Guest House, Hirakud on 12, 13, June, 99 for the Industrial Relations Officers of NCLPs (National Child Labour Projects) of Sambalpur Division.

2. Regional training-cum-workshop on accounting practices in National Child Labour Projects of Orissa and West Bengal was organised by State Labour Institute on 26-29th July, 99 at Bhubaneswar.

3. ILO sponsored preparatory meeting on Child Labour in Orissa was held at Garden Inn, Bhubaneswar on 26th and 27th August' 99.

4. A workshop-cum-training programme for sensiting the N.G.O. for operation of 60 child labour prevention centres in 7 super cyclone affected districts of Orissa was held from 27.2.2000 to 29.2.2000. The training was organised jointly by UNICEF, V.V. Giri NLI and State Labour Institute at Hotel Prachi, Bhubaneswar.

5. A workshop training on effective enforcement of labour was of the ALOS and RLIs the Labour Directorate was organised by State Labour Institute and V.V. Giri National Labour Institute, Noida at Hotel Keshari, Bhubaneswar from 20.12.99 to 24.12.99.

6. A workshop-cum-training for the field officer, Officers of labour Directorate belonging to 7 super cyclone affected districts was jointly organised by V.V. Giri, NLI and State Labour Institute from 1.3.2000 to 2.3.2000 at Hotel Keshari, Bhubaneswar for operation of 60 child labour prevention centre.

7. A review meeting on the pace and progress of the National Child Labour Projects (NCLPs) operating in Orissa was conducted by Dr. L. Mishra, I.A.S. Orissa Secretariat on 6.4.2000 at Bhubaneswar. The Project Director of 18 NCLPs, the Collector of Ganjam, Angul, Balasore, Cuttack, Labour and Employment Deptt. Labour Commissioner, Joint Labour Commissioner, Dy. Director State Labour Institute at Jt. Director Ministry of Labour participated in the said meeting.

8. 9 days, training programme for instructors of 60 child labour prevention centres functioning in the

Super Cyclone district of Puri, Khurda, Cuttack, Jagatsinghpur, Jajpur, Kendrapara and Bhadrak was organised by State Labour Institute at Hotel Prachi, Bhubaneswar from 1.6.2000 to 9.6.2000.

9. A five day training programme of effective labour law enforcement for Labour Inspectors/Labour Enforcement Officer of Orissa was jointly organised by the State Labour Institute and V.V. Giri National Labour Institute at Bhubaneswar from 11-15 September, 2000.

10. One day workshop for 60 NGOs operating Child Labour Prevention Centre was organised in the conference hall of the Labour Director, Orissa, Bhubaneswar on 20.9.2000. This programme was jointly organised by the UNICEF and State Labour Institute.

11. District Level and Block level Social mobilisation programmes against engagement of child labour was organised jointly by the UNICEF and State Labour Institute in the Districts of Angul, Phulbani, Mayurbhanj, Rayagada, Bolangir and Sambalpur during October and November 2000.

All of these seminars and workshops proved to be high expensive but results are far from satisfaction. It is hypothetical to say that had the children continued to be in the school, there would not have the practice of child labour in this hazardous works'! Establishment "Bala Sevashrama" must be required at every block level for prohibiting them to work in this hazard occupation. Road permit of the vehicle must be cancelled of those who employ child labour. A suitable policy should also be launched to help prevention of child labour and assists to their parents, as they required.

It is clearly says that while some healthy work habit in childhood may be a social good and Nation gains in future but child labour itself is a great social evil and a national wastage.

"The economic necessity for wage earning to support the family deprives the child of opportunities for education, whole some play and recreations stunts his physical growth, interferes with the normal development of his personality and thwarts his preparations for adult responsibility".

What is responsible for this?

It is the Govt.?

Employer?

Or we?

We have also blocked our future generation from their healthy progress.

References

1. *Labour Statistics in Orissa, 2000* by the Labour Commissioner, Orissa, 2000.
2. Dr. Bhogoliwal T.N. *"Economic of Labour and Industrial Relation"*. pp. 1-3, 613-618.
3. Dr. Sahu, Bhagawan *"Aska in the History and Culture of Orissa"* "Souvenir" of VI Annual Conference Ganjam Economics Seminar 1993, pp. No. 1-4.

5

Indian Child Labour: Challenges for 21st Century

***Pradeepta K. Samanta**
****Ashok Kumar Mohanty**

Introduction

Worldover, child labour is recognized as a social evil. It detracts children from essential activities like leisure, play and education, which are indispensable for their normal growth and dignified and existence. According to Homerfloks, Chairman, Unites States National Labour Committee, child labour is defined as any work by children that interferes with their full physical development, their opportunities for desirable minimum of education or their needed recreation. A child is mechanised to do a given work silently against his/her wish and what is worse at a very nominal wage in an incongenial atmosphere. The existence of child labour

* Mr. Pradeepta K. Samanta, Research Scholar; and

** Dr. Ashok Kumar Mohanty, Reader and Head, P.G. Department of Commerce, Berhampur University, Berhampur—760 007 (Orissa).

deprives a nation of its potential worker of future who could have been more productive if not forced to work in their childhood. The Statistics Bureau Report 1996 of the ILO estimated that there were 250 million child labour in the world out of which 120 million were working as full time and 130 million as part time worker.[1] Asia account's for an alarming projection of 61.2 per cent followed by Africa 32 per cent and Latin America 6.8 per cent. In India, the number of child labour has been reduced from 13.60 million (6% of total workforce) in 1981 to 11.30 million (3.51% of total workforce) in 1991. But the World Bank Report of January, 2000 has revealed that there are 80 million working children in India of which 15 million are bonded working children. Besides the disquieting fact of phenomenal increase in the number of child labour in a period of just one decade, the report points out that the child labourers in India are forced to join the works ranging from prostitution to hazardous occupations.[2] There is no dearth of legislation's in the country to combat the menace of child labour; poverty, uneven development, low level of education, etc., though are usually attributed to this growing practice, states like Tamil Nadu, Andhra Pradesh even on high growth trajectory exhibit higher incidence of child labour. Attempts are made in this chapter to analyse in detail the ramification of the problem of child labour, measures both government and non-governmental legislation and otherwise taken so far and what else are ought to be done to eradicate the ghostly menace of child labour from India particularly when the country enters 21st century with the pride of having world class scientific and technological manpower.

Definitions of Child Labour

In common parlance, child labour is the work, which involves some degree of exploitation i.e. physical, mental, economic and hence impairs the health and development of children. The Encyclopaedia of Social Science defines a child labour as any work done by a child himself/herself directly or indirectly who has not completed the fourteenth year of age. The Concerned for Working Children (CWC), a Bangalore-based group defines a child labourer as a person who has not completed his/her fifteenth year of age and is working with or without wage/income on part time or full time basis. According to UNICEF, any child out of school is a child labour. But in terms of priority of action, it is imperative to abolish the most exploitative and most intolerable forms of child labour as a first priority. In the context of exploitation, UNICEF has given a comprehensive formulation in its attempt at defining child labour.

1. Starting full time work at too early an age.
2. Working too long within or outside the family and unable to attend school.
3. Work on the street is unhealthy and dangerous.
4. Too much responsibility at too early an age as in the domestic situation where children under 18 may have to look after younger brothers and sisters for a whole day, there by foregoing school attendance.
5. Inadequate remuneration for working outside the family as in the case of child workers in carpet weaving industry.

Hence, children not attending fourteen years of age engaged in work both domestic or outside in incongenial and exploitative environment, thus being deprived of attending school, are regarded as child labourers.

Causes of Child Labour

Socio-economic factors are primarily responsible for perpetuation of child labour in developing and developed countries. Wide spread and chronic economic poverty in developing world forces parents to send their children for work. Casteism, gender discrimination, large family size low level of income, geographically disadvantaged area, illiteracy etc., do contribute significantly to the cause of child labour practice. Further, with advantages like low remuneration, not unionised, no demand for overtime, simple and easy to be moulded and punished etc., being inherent with children, employers in this industrialised and scientific era prefer child labour. In most underdeveloped and agrarian society children are part of labour force. With the growth of industrialisation, they are moving from families to factories.

Adverse Consequences of Child Labour

A large number of children working in different industries and factories do suffer from malnutrition which eventually lower their resistance and makes them all the more vulnerable to diseases. Carrying heavy loads and working in cramped spaces in factory causes deformity particularly of bones and hinders general growth. Owing to unhygienic working conditions several jobs expose children to various kinds of health hazards due to extensive use of chemicals and poisonous substances in industries and pollutants discharged by them. Long hours of works in such working conditions obviously endanger children's physical health and mental growth leading to occupational health problem. A study carried out in Japan showed a difference of 4 cms in height between those who began work before the age of 14 and those after 18 years, whereas, their height was comparable at the age of 12 years.[3]

Major Forms of Child Labour

The child labour exists in the following forms:

1. Domestic works like cleaning, cooking, childcare and other chores to which children are subjected to in almost all types of societies.

2. Children engaged in subsistence activities which are non-domestic but non-monetary like engagement in

farms, collection of fuel, water, etc. in agrarian economies.

3. Bonded labour is the most exploitative from of child labour.

4. Wage employment is another type of child labour where children are engaged in employment either as part of a family group or individually in agricultural worksites, domestic services, manufacturing and services activities.

5. Child labour is also involved in marginal work, like work of a short term or irregular nature like selling news papers, shoe shining, looking after cars, garbage collection and sorting out objects from garbages.

6. There is another category of child labour that lacks access to school or is a drop out from the school. Such children having no employment/engagement, enter into idleness or irregular and some times antisocial activities. Many of such children are found engaged in theft, prostitution and other socially undesirable or illegal activities.

Child Labour: Global Scene

Despite the fact that world has witnessed phenomenal progress due to spectacular growth in science and technology and more particularly due to information technology towards the end of 20th century, the problem of child labour still remains intractable in many parts of the globe. Though the problem is chronic in developing third world countries, the developed countries are not free from the malaise. In the U.K., more than one million under age children work illegally. The USA has also about 8 lakh children working in various fields. In the densely populated poor and developing countries the child labour problem is passing through a miserable state.

Out of 250 million child labour (ILO—1996), Asia represents 61.2 per cent, Africa 32 per cent and Latin America 6.86 per cent of child labour. The ILO study also reveals that 11 to 20 per cent of work forces in the third world countries are child labour.[4] A large number of them are found hazardous industries such as mining, fire works manufacturing, leather tanning etc.

Child Labour: Indian Scenario

Legislative and Other Supportive Measures in India to Combat Child Labour

The Government of India, realising the gravity of the problem of child labour in the country has initiated steps ranging from making constitutional provisions to enactment of various legislation and Acts to make the country free from the menace of child labour. Article 24 of Indian Constitution provides that no child below the age of 14 years shall be employed in any factory, or mine or other hazardous occupations or work. Article 31 envisages that the state shall endeavour to provide in its policy specially to ensure that youthful age of children is not abused and they are not forced to accept an employment detrimental to their age and physical ability owing to any economic compulsion. Children are to be provided opportunities to develop their faculties in a healthy manner and in free and respectful situations. They are to be protected against exploitation of their childhood and youth and against moral or physical abandonment. Article 45 envisages free and compulsory education for children. The Child Labour (Prohibition and Regulation) Act 1986 is an important legislation that seeks to prohibit child labour in certain industries designated as hazardous and regulate working conditions in other areas of employment. This Act prohibits employment of children in 12 occupations and 51 hazardous processes. It also provides for an expansion of this list on the advice of the Child Labour Technical Advisory Committee and for the protection of working children not employed in notified hazardous occupations. The Government of India formulated the National Child Labour Policy in 1987 under which provisions have been made to launch project based actional plan in child labour endemic area to deal with the problem. The National Agenda for Governance (1998) of the NDA government contains provisions like rehabilitation measures, implementation of National Child Labour Projects, grants in aid to voluntary agencies and international programme for the Elimination of Child Labour, etc., to effectively combat the evil of child labour practices in the country. The Govt. of India also has instituted different study groups and committees like Harbans Singh Committee, Gurapad Swami Committee, Sanat Mehta Committee, Singvi Committee to make valuable suggestions to deal with the problem of child labour. The Ministry of Human Resource Development operates a major programme for promotion of education among children compelled to work due to poverty through Non-Formal Education (NFE) centres. The clientele for NFE are identified as children of a location without school, school drop outs, working children and girls who can not attend school. The National Policy on Education NPE (1986) emphasizes the importance of continuing non-formal education for working children. Commencement of the scheme of well defined Open Learning System (OLS), starting of day care centres, provisions of free uniform, mid-day meals, text books, stationary and coordination of support services such as drinking water, fodder and fuel to release children especially girls as well as women from related domestic chores in the Ninth Five Year Plan (1997-2000) of the Government are intended to overcome the malady of child labour in the country.

Present State in India

In India, the problem of child labour is infact, catastrophic. Today the country is having the world's largest number of child labour. According to a UN estimate, of every three world's working children, one is from India. As per 1991 census, there were 11.3 million child labour in the country, but the World Banks Report of January 2000 has put the figure of child labour in India at 80 million representing more than 6 fold rise in a period of just one decade. If one goes by the UNICEF report of 1997 which has estimated world child labour population at 250 million, over one third are found in India.[5] Thus the fast growing population of child labour is a matter of grave concern for India which needs to be addressed urgently with all sincerity. Another disturbing matter is child labour is found in almost all parts of India performing a variety of jobs. They work in the match stick and fire work industries of Sivakasi in Tamil Nadu, diamond polishing industry of Surat in Gujarat, precious stone polishing industry in Jaipur (Rajasthan), glass industry of Forezabad, brass-ware industry of Moradabad, Carpet industry of Mirzapur and Bhadohi, lock-making industry in Aligarh, State industry of Mandasaur, Madhya Pradesh and Markapur, Andhra Pradesh. Besides, a significant number of Child labour is also found in the unorganised, informal and unregulated sectors of the economy. The urorganised sector accounts for a whole army of child labour working as domestic servants, helpers or assistants in restaurants, hotels, way side shops, dhabhas, canteens, hawkers, paper vendors, porters, shoeshine boys, scavengers, assistants in small shops, repair shops and helpers at construction sites engaged in breaking stones, unloading goods, etc.[6] Many are engaged with their parents as companions and helpers in agricultural farms and conventional industrial occupations. Employed children are seen in wood carving works, mining sector, leather tanneries, beedi making etc. Analysis of India's 1991 census also reveals that among various states, Andhra Pradesh tops the list by containing 17 lakhs of working children. The other states having more than 10 lakh working children are Uttar Pradesh (14.10 lakh), Madhya Pradesh (13.52 lakh) and Maharashtra (10.68 lakh). States like Karnataka, Bihar, Rajasthan and West Bengal also contain high number of child labour ranging between 7 to 10 lakh.[7] Another disquieting trend is as revealed from a study by National Social Institute, New Delhi on Child Labour, nearly 80 per cent of all children belonging to the Scheduled Caste/Tribes have been exploited and marginalised in India for centuries.

The Government of India has prepared an action plan to tackle the problem of child labour by 2007.[8] With a view to rehabilitating child labour, special schools and centres have been set up where there is provision of informal education, vocational training, nutrition etc., for children relieved from work under National Child Labour Programme (NCLP). So far 1044 schools in 106 districts in the country have been set up. Most of such schools and beneficiaries are in the states of Andhra Pradesh and Orissa. The Government of India has also proposals to set up committees of mothers from DWCRA (Development of Women and Children in the Rural Areas) groups to tackle the problem of child labour. Workshops are being organised to discuss various problems confronting child labourers at regional levels and to suggest remedial measures to bring them into the national mainstream.

Conclusion

Children are the future of a nation. While healthy, prosperous and growing children ensure bright future, working, exploited and physically weak children not only suffer but also fail to contribute towards the growth of the country. Studies reveal that though child labour is primarily an outcome of poverty and uneven development, no country in the world today is free from the menace of child labour. Every country rich or poor, developed or developing, technologically advanced or not endeavours to eliminate or reduce the plight of the child labour as none of them could afford to bear the brunt of mortgaging the future by ignoring the working children. The Government of India, since the adoption of constitution in 1950 has been making efforts to tackle the problems of child labour in the country. There has been no dearth of Legislation's and Acts, committees and commissions, policies and programmes both at government and non-governmental levels but the miseries of working children go unabated. Though there has been reduction in the number of working children between 1981 and 1991 census, the decade of 90, India experiences a phenomenal rise in their number. World Bank report of January 2000, put the figure at 80-million child labour, nearly one third of world's working children. The Government of India, State Governments, International Agencies like UNICEF, ILO and World Bank, and non-governmental agencies (NGOs) are engaged in the country by way of enforcements of Children Labour Act, Minimum Wage Act etc., implementation of various poverty alleviation and employment generation programmes for parents, setting up of specific school under National Child Labour Programme (NCLP) etc., for identification, rehabilitation and upliftment of child labour. Most of the developed countries have predicted India to become a superpower in 21st Century. But India being a member of WTO sees threats in the international markets in respect of products like textile, gems, beedi, carpets, etc., using child labour. Hence protection of child labour is not only required for preserving country's future valuable human resource, but also to promote Indian dominance in world economy.

References

1. International Labour Organisation (ILO), *Bureau of Statistics Report 1996*.
2. Bhandari J., "Child Labour: The Challenges Ahead", *Yojana*, Vol. 44, No. 9, New Delhi, September, 2000, pp. 40-41.
3. Shah P.M., "Child Labour—A Threat to Health and Development, *Defence for Children International*, 2nd Rev. Edn, Geneva, 1985.
4. International Labour Organisation (ILO). *op. cit.*
5. Jha S.M. "Social Regulations for Child Labourers", *Employment News*, New Delhi, October, 4-10, 1997, p. 1.

6. Kanbargi R (Ed), Child Labour in Indian Subcontinent—Dimensions and Implications, Sage Publications, New Delhi, 1991, p. 4.

7. Government of India, "*All Indian Census Report—1991*", New Delhi, 1994.

8. "Action Plan to solve Child Labour Problem by 2007", *The Hindu*, Vol. 123, No. 302, Visakhapatnam, 21st December 2000, p. 3.

ANNEXTURE—1

Sl. No.	*Occupation*	*Health Hazards*
1.	Carpet weaving	— Asthma, spiral Problems, loss of appetite, cuts
2.	Gem polishing	— Eye strains, Stiffness of limbs
3.	Zari Embroidery	— Spondylitis, lead poisoning
4.	Stone and slate quarries	— Silicosis, Asthma, Tuberculosis
5.	Glass and bangle making	— Burns and cuts, bronchitis, silicosis
6.	Match and fire-work making	— Burns, dizziness, severe back and neck pains
7.	Rag-picking	— Tetanus and skin diseases
8.	Construction work	— Body injuries from falls and carry heavy weights
9.	Agriculture	— Cuts and injuries from sharp farm implements dizziness and asthma caused by fumes from pesficides and fertilizers

(Contd...)

10.	Domestic work	— Accidents, cuts and burns
11.	Powerloom weaving	— Byssinosis leading to bronchitis and tuberculosis
12.	Pottery workers	— Asthmatic bronchitis, tuberculosis, pneumoconious lung disorders, potassium cyanide poisoning
13.	Lock making	— Electric shocks.

6

Child Labour in Southern Orissa—A Study

*Dr. Pradeep Kumar Pattanayak

The National Policy for children, 1971 envisages the state to provide adequate service both before and after birth and enough the period of growth to ensure their full physical, mental and social development.

The Convention on the Rights of the Child (CRC) declared that the state bodies recognize that every child has the inherent right to life. The state parties shall ensure to the maximum extent possible, the survival and development of the child.

Children are the blooming flowers in the garden of society and the future of our nation. In every minute 5/6 childrens are dying in the world. The child population is 1/10th of the population of the whole world. According to the report of U.N.O., the child mortality rate is very high in India

* Dr. Pradeep Kumar Pattanayak is a Lecturer in Economics, K.D. Science College, Pochilima, Dist.: Ganjam.

as well as in Orissa 22.45 crores of the child population are constituting work-force in the world. 6.22 million of the child population are engaged as child labour in various industries, shop, restaurant, hotel etc. in India. They are no better than the animals. The child labour are tortured in all aspects by their masters, while in the work.

Southern Orissa comprises four districts before 1st, October, 1992 but, after that the state Government has decided to this region to ten districts, viz., Ganjam, Gajapati, Rayagada, Koraput, Malkangiri, Nawrangapur, Kalahandi, Naupada, Phulabani and Boudh. The geographical land area of the region is about 62.383 sq. kms. which is 40 per cent of the geographical land area of the region is approximately 86, 35,598 lakhs, which is 27 per cent of the population of Orissa. The total forest area covered 47.5 per cent in the state. The literacy rate is 26.35 per cent and the male and female literacy rate is 41.30 per cent and 23.25 per cent respectively. The schedule caste and schedule tribe population having 49.59 per cent in the state. 50 per cent of the people are living below the poverty line (BPL) in Southern Orissa in the state.

The Southern Orissa comprises of 15 sub-division, 46 tahasils, 101 community development block, 117 police station, 1954 Gram Panchayat alongwith 16,615 total villages. There are 41 town including 6 municipalities and 32 N.A.C. The whole region is headed by Revenue Divisional Commissioner (RDC) in Southern Orissa.

The child labourers are working in various types of regular employment in southern Orissa, undertake activities ranging from agriculture and livestock to forestry, plantation, orchards, mining and quarrying, manufacturing, processing, construction, trade and commerce transport, storage, communication, weaving, hotels and restaurants etc. However, more than 5 lakhs children are working in the aforesaid activities in southern Orissa. Mostly they are working for 12 to 15 hours daily their various work activities. However more than 80 per cent of children work primarily as agricultural labour and cultivators. But, in hotel and restaurant, rice mill and brick industry they are paid very low wages per day. The Table—6.1 shows the vivid picture of child labour in ten districts of southern Orissa.

Table—6.1 Child Labour in Southern Orissa (1999 to 2000)

Sl. No.	*Name of the district*	*Total no. of child labour*	*No. of percentage*
1.	Ganjam	75,887	27.68
2.	Gajapati	15,684	5.72
3.	Rayagada	24,432	8.91
4.	Koraput	35,962	13.11
5.	Malakanagiri	13,832	5.04
6.	Nowrangapur	29,052	10.59
7.	Kalahandi	35,675	13.01
8.	Nuapada	15,000	5.47
9.	Kandhamal	18,263	6.66
10.	Boudh	10,350	3.77
	Total	**2,74,138**	**100**

Source : Labour Bureau, Bhubaneswar.

The Table—6.1 reveals the 27.68 per cent of child worker to total is highest in the Ganjam district and the 3.77 per cent lowest in Boudh district in southern Orissa. While in order to first, second and third position of the child workers 27.68 per cent in Ganjam, 13.11 per cent in Koraput and 13.01 per cent in Kalahandi district respectively in southern Orissa. The official record shows the total number of child worker are 2,74,138. But the number is much more as per non-official estimates.

Natural endowments such as minerals, metals, stone and weaving, marine products, brick industry and glass works etc., have led to economic activities providing employment to locally skilled and unskilled child worker in southern Orissa. The child workers are mostly working in the urban area to get more wages such as, Berhampur, Rayagada, Bhawanipatna, Parlakhemundi, Kesinga, Dhermagarh, Aska, Phulbani, Boudh, Chatrapur, Jeypore, Sunabedha, Koraput, Bhanjanagar, Balliguda, Umerkota and various N.A.C. and Semi-urban areas in southern Orissa. The examples of such areas in southern Orissa are weaving in Ganjam district silk work in Berhampur, marine in Gopalpur. Granites in Ganjam, minor forest produce are belong to, collection of Kendu leaves, as Bidi making and leave products in the tribal district such as Phulbani, Koraput, Rayagada, Gajapati, Nowarangapur and Malakanagiri etc.

In rural areas girl children work mainly a agricultural workers. Girls are involved in animals and farm operations. Such as, sowing, transplanting, weeding, harvesting, sortings and grading. In urban areas they are mainly employed in occupations such as house work, Bidi making, Agarbati making and also in the match industry.

There are various occupations which results in health hazardous to child labourers. In agriculture, children suffer from exhaustion, de-hydration, headache and are exposed to hazardous pesticides, tetanus, geliena worm, intestation and hook-worm, unclean and unsafe drinking water, cause amolbiasis, thyphoid, dysentery, cholera and serious infective hepatitis. It is observed in some places in both rural and urban area. The child labourers are sexually exploited in artificial manner and involved to them in the sex work in 'Dhaba' hotel of National Highway roadsides.

The following legislative support by central laws and Government policies are such as The Children (pledging of labour) Act, 1933, The Child Labour (Prohibition and

Regulation Act) 1986. Similarly, the Government Policy are as follows, viz., National Policy for Children 1974, National Policy on Child Labour 1987. The Government of India is implements more than 120 schemes and programmes for welfare and development of children and women.

Several voluntary organisations and non-governmental organisations have taken keen interest about the Child Labour Rehabilitation Project under the banner of National Child Labour Project in various districts in southern Orissa viz., Ganjam, Gajapati, Kalahandi, Phulbani, Koraput and Malkangiri etc. But the government funds are manipulates by several voluntary organisations, complained by local residents.

Employing children below and upto 14 years of age for work is reprehensible, more so, by a government servant as such children are subjected to inhuman treatment and long hours of duty, the National Human Rights Commission says.

Above all the problems of the child labourers in southern Orissa they are living below standard and deprived the rights of the society. They are exploited in physically, mentally, sexually and financially by their masters. The following suggestion may adopt in Government policy in the above problem of child labour are mentioned below.

- To proper identify the number of child in each block and village in Orissa.
- To make and adopt a strong and suitable plan by the Government for eradication of the problem.
- To abolish the system, implement strong action to the person, those who violates the law.
- To impart and implement the compulsory education up to 10th class.
- To establish a child rights commission in the state.

- To create awareness among the people through seminar, workshop, padayatra and exhibition.
- To proper co-ordinate between government and voluntary organisations in the child labour project.
- To imprison and fine the culprits in criminal cases, those who violate the laws.
- To make a monitoring cell in each block in the State to protect the child labour through N.S.S., N.C.C. and scout and guide volunteers.

References

1. Economic Survey (Orissa) 1997-98.
2. Labour Minister Conference Report 17th May, 1993.
3. Dharitri (chhutidina) 29 November- 5 December, 1998.
4. Times of India, 23rd November, 1999.
5. Dharitri (A daily Oriya) 10th July, 2000.
6. Samaya (A daily Oriya) 28th December, 2000.

7

Child Labour in Hazardous Occupation: A Study of India and Orissa

*R.L. Panigrahy

Introduction

Employment of child labour is an age old civilisation. In Manusmriti and Arthasastra, there are mentions of child labour and protection of children. Children at very tender age of 4 to 14 years at work as labourers is known as child labour.

Thus child labour may be defined as "children are forced to work as labour for the sake of earning a livelihood. They are better substitutes of adult labourers. The child labourers are always blamed not working. People always search such cheap labour force to work.

* Mr. Panigrahy is working as a Faculty in the Department of Computer Science and Commerce, Science College, Hinjilicut—761 102, Ganjam, Orissa.

Child labour is defined as a person who has not completed the age of 14 years of age according to Child Labour (Prohibition and Regulation) Act 1986, here the age factor is par in Minimum Wages Act 1948, Plantation Act 1951, Merchant Shipping Act 1958, Motor Transport Act, 1961. At present the total estimate of child labour is more than 250 million (ILO estimates) out of which 120 million are less than 6 years and 2 million are engaged in hazardous occupations like carpet work, glass work, fire works, chemical industries, etc. As per UN estimate, of every 5 children working, 1 is from India.

The existence of child labour in South East Asia and Asian countries has become a matter of international concern during the present decade. More than 80 per cent of the working children in Asia belong to the rural areas and in unorganised primary sector of the economy.

Table—7.1 Distribution of Child Labour in the Globe

Continents	*No. (in millions)*	*% share in total*
South East Asia	29.0	55.77
Rest of Asia	9.1	17.50
Africa	9.7	18.65
South (Latin) America	3.1	5.96
Europe	0.7	1.34
North America	0.3	0.59
Oceania	0.1	0.19
World total	**52.0**	**100.00**

Causes of Child Labour

Poverty

The grinding poverty is the main cause of child to be

forced to become labourer by which people can get cheap labour force. The poverty may be mainly divided in 5 categories.

1. *Economic Poverty:* Inadequate financial resource including income, which does not meet the day-to-day expenses even if basic amenities of life of a family which create economic poverty.

2. *Geographical Poverty:* Certain communities are located in such a geographical are being deprived of where there is no scope of natural resources and supportive infrastructure for economic development of the community.

3. *Social Poverty:* It is a product of gender, caste, class.

4. *Cultural Poverty:* It is the poverty created by belief, faith, culture, caste, etc.

5. *Political Poverty:* Due to no political access and representation, it creates poverty which cause child labour.

In spite of poverty, there are several causes of child labour are:

(i) poverty in which children can help their family;

(ii) to meet the expenses of family in case of diseased parents;

(iii) to meet the expenses of deceased family;

(iv) to meet the long standing debt recovery;

(v) to meet the expenses of family due to sudden death or paralysis of the head of bread winner of the family;

(vi) due to personal or caste exploitation;

(vii) due to no parents and relatives;

(viii) due to huge size of family;

(ix) due to bad habits of parents like drinking, gambling, etc.

(x) due to laziness of parents to work.

Causes of Child Labour in Orissa

In this context, Labour Directorate of Orissa has surveyed and prepare a report of causes of child labour as.

Table—7.2 Causes and Percentages of Child Labour in Orissa

Cause	*% of child labour (both sexes)*
Poverty	54
Children's desire to work	18
Big size of family	12
Parent's inability to provide education	8
Death of parents	4
Accident of father and less earning capacity	2
Total	**100**

Source : Orissa Review, May-June, 1997, p. 40.

Child Labour in Comparison to Orissa

Child labour also created in an agrarian country, less developed over populated country. The problem of child labour is more acute in rural India as well as in Orissa. There is 82 per cent of majority child labour found in agrarian sector and 18 per cent among industries in Orissa. The female child is ¼th of the total child labour belongs to urban sector. Child labour is more than all India average of 91.14 per cent.

Child labour in developed districts of Orissa is in a miserable conditions where Cuttack is in highest position and Kandhamal (Phulbani) is in lowest.

Table—7.3 Child Labour in District-wise

District name	*No. of child labour*
Cuttack	700
Sambalpur	600
Dhenkanal	400
Puri	200
Bolangir	150
Koraput	61
Keonjhor	24
Kalahandi	22
Kandhamal (Phulbani)	4

Source : Orissa Review, May-June, 1997 p. 41.

Table—7.4 Child Labour in Rural Areas of Selected States

Name of the States	*% of Child Labour*
1	**2**
Arunachal Pradesh	98.24
Jammu and Kashmir	96.90
Nagaland	95.88
Madhya Pradesh	94.58
Tripura	94.79

(Contd...)

1	2
Bihar	94.97
Orissa	94.79
Sikkim	93.64

Source : Orissa Review, May-June' 1997 p. 41.

Table—7.5 Child Labour to Total Work Force

State name	*% of child labour to total work force*
Andhra Pradesh	7.75
Karnataka	7.08
Orissa	5.79
Lakshadeep	0.39

Source : Orissa Review, May-June, 1997, p. 41.

Employment of Child Labour

Child labour is still concentrated in Beedi making, brick kilns, weaving, hotel and restaurants, vehicles' workshops, garages, shops, forestry, fishing, mining, quarrying, households, plucking of kendu leaves, collection of seeds, mahula, siali leaves, bakeries, match industries, storage and transport and communication services, graphites, soap and detergents, assembling of small machinery shops, fine works, etc.

It is a fact to be admitted that a country which can not find jobs for 36 million adults being unemployed where there is 44 million children get space for employment. Child labour is not caused by poverty but it is cheap and easy to get.

Child Labour in Hazardous Occupation

People search for cheap labour that is only possible in case of child labour shows. Most of the working children are found in unorganised sector and in marginal occupation on the street. The problems of urban child labour are analysed as 10 kinds of economic activities like domestic work, non-domestic work, non-monetary work, bonded labour, schooling, idleness and unemployment, recreation and leisure and productive activities. Most of the child labour engaged in urban are smuggling and begging. Millions of child labour are forced labour and millions are bonded. It is also including the children kidnapped as well as who are otherwise lured away from their families to be imprisoned sweatshops or brothels. The sexual exploitation of children is now a new feature of economic life in several countries are prepared by ECPAT. In a news letter of July' 1993, ECPAT reported that 31 countries were sexual abuses estimated in 1 million child prostitutes in Asia out of which 4 lakhs are in India. So, the child labour should get protected from this and whatever is harmful to his health or physical, mental, spiritual, moral and social development. The society and Govt. should protect the child from all forms of sexual exploitations and sexual abuses. In spite of this unfortunately the child labourers are engaged in the hazardous occupations are to dragged out and the employers of child labour should alert on the legal points.

Protection of Child Labour from Hazardous Occupation

Child labour is not illegal in India, but the exploitation, hazardous occupations are to be prohibited and restricted legally. Hence, Govt. also taken certain legal amendments as follows:

Article 14 of Indian Constitution prescribes that no child under 14 years should be made to work in any factory or a mine or engage in any other hazardous employment.

Article 39 (e) directs the state to see that the tender age children are not abused and that citizens are not compelled by economic circumstances to do work that is unsuited to their age or strength.

Article 39 (f) emphasises that the need to say that childhood and young are protected against exploitation and against moral and material detriment.

Article 23 confers a fundamental right against certain forms of exploitation. The provision of punishment for such exploitations are provided in Indian Penal Code.

Article 15(3) has special provisions for women and children.

Article 45 (DPSP) says that the state shall endeavour to provide within a period of 10 years from the commencement of the constitution free and compulsory education for all children until they complete the age of 15 years.

Child Labour (Prohibition and Protection) Act 1986 prohibits child labour in certain occupations.

Factories Act 1948 defines minimum age of employment fixed to 14 years and 5 hours work, employment during night and on hazardous occupations was prescribed.

Mines Act 1952 defines minimum age of employment in mines is fixed at 15, below age children may be employed for part time or in any open excavation.

Plantation Act 1957 fixed age of employment at 12 years.

Employment of Child Labour Act 1938 was to check abuses arising out of employment in workshops which are outside the scope of factory legislation. Employment of child between 15 and 17 during night in railways and port is prohibited.

The Motor Transport Workers Act 1961 also prohibits employment of children between 14 years.

Remedies of Child Labour

Integrated Child Labour Development Service (ICDS) scheme has left much emphasis on the establishment of linkage between education and childhood care which are mainly located in rural and tribal areas aiming to educate and taking care of children. In almost all blocks of India ICDS schemes are going on.

The National Policy for Children (NPC) started in 7th plan emphasised the importance of free and compulsory education for all children upto the age of 14, provisions of health and nutritional programmes and services, providing alternative forms of education for children unable to take full advantage of formal school education and measures for protecting children against neglect, cruelty and exploitations. The Commissions of Labour Standards has recommended National Policy of Child Labour (NPCL) need to adopt the goal by the parliament to end all forms of child labour by 2010 A.D. and launch the campaign under ILO/UNESCO. The commission also estimated 25 million child labour force in country is growing each year which is 4 per cent, it needs Rs. 15,000 crores to abolish it totally. The commission also have the report of 150 industries of non-hazardous for children to work.

There is a Campaign Against Child Labour (CACL) set up in 1992, a society taking initiative to eradicate child labour. In order to reach the goal, the CACL tries to disseminate information in Children's rights to create public awareness while simultaneously working with child labourers and their parents to sensise them about their rights.

In spite of the above explanations, the community as a whole should try to eradicate child labour and should treat it as one of responsibility which drag our nation from the list of lower standards in the world scenario.

References

Social Welfare, Feb. 1996

1. *"Child Labour Education is a Key"*—U.K. Das.
2. *"Child Labour Problems and Solutions"*—Prof. K.L. Tiwari.
3. *"Child Labour Issues and Laws"*—Dr. D.V. Rao and Prof. B.Y. Raju.
4. *"Child Labour Adults at the Age of Five"*—Mrs. A. Suhara.
5. *"Child Prostitutes and Sex Tourism"*—Dr. L.M. Mital.
6. *"New Diary-Call to Adopt National Policy on Child Labour"* PTI, New Delhi.

Social Welfare, Apr. 1996

7. *"Gender Perspective in Child Labour"*—Dr. Neeti Mohanti.
8. *"Restoring Childhood to Child Labour"*—Uma Joshi.

Social Welfare, Dec. 1995

9. *"ICDS Scheme Need Revamping"*—Uma Joshi.
10. *"Report Colombo Conference—The Girl Child Especially in Different Circumstances"*—B. Bhamati.
11. *"Rights of Child—Role of the Media"*—Rita Puhani.

Social Welfare, Mar., 1996

12. *"Guarding the Girl Child"*—Dr. I. Satya Sundaram

Orissa Review, May-June, 1997

13. *"Child Labour in Orissa Today"*—Dr. H.K. Misra.
14. *Vision* Sep. -December. 1998.

Economics of Child and Industrial Relations, 1996 Edition—Dr. T.N. Bhagoliwal

15. Chapter—26 *"Child and Women Labour"*
16. Chapter—29 *"Labour Policy in India"*

8

Child Labour in Hazardous Engagements—A Focus on the N.C.L.P. in Bolangir

***Dr. Surendra Kumar Padhy**
****Mr. Ashok Kumar Panda**

Introduction

Scholars and Researchers have left no room to scan out and suggest on the problems associated with child labour. Children of today's world are no doubt the adults of tomorrow to gear up the growth potentialities of each country. Its, therefore, obligatory for any nation to pay due attention on the physical and mental growth of its children. Researchers are of the opinion that many children start working because of illiteracy, poverty, lack of awareness or compulsion. The World Bank Report of January 2000 has been a matter of

* Dr. Surendra Kumar Padhy is working as a Senior Lecturer in Commerce, D.A.V College, Titlagarh in Orissa.

** Mr. Ashok Kumar Panda, Senior Lecturer in Commerce D.A.V. College, Titilagarh District Bolangir concern for all the Developing Countries in general and for India in particular. The reports ranks India at the top of the list of countries where the density of working children is the maximum. More distressing fact in the report relates to the bonded working children, which is estimated to be one-fourth of the total working children in the country. Still threatening is the statistics relating to the country's children under hazardous engagements. The International Labour Organisation (ILO) Report, 1975; The National Statistical Survey (NSS) during 1977-78; The Indian Planning Commission's Report, 1983; The Report of the Operation Research Group, Baroda, 1983; The Indian Census, 1981; The Labour Force and Planning Commission Report, 1995; ILO Report 1996 and The UNICEF Report, 1997 are the few sources of supplying data on the children of the country working under hazardous and non-hazardous environments. However, it is difficult to state the accurate figure for the child labour in the country. The difficulty in collecting data on child labour may be attributed to the facts like international disclosure of biased informations for fear of prosecutions, migration of child workers, temporary absence of child workers during the period of survey etc.

Over the years, the State of Orissa has been considered as a backward state in the country. The economic condition of the people in the state is very miserable. Still worse is the financial condition of the people of Bolangir district where most of the members of a family work to earn only a square meal a day. District Bolangir is one of the identified "Most Backward KBK District" of Orissa. The district is exposed to serious drought, and the people of this district are habituated of going to the neighbouring states in search of employment. The prospective employers of the neighbouring states consider it to be an opportunity and attract the innocent people of this district with a meagre advance towards payment of wages. These employers take interest on the people of Bolangir district because they know that these people move along with all their family members where they find no difficulty in putting the child workers into hazardous occupations. Moreover, these employers get more return out of the wages they pay to these child workers. Thus, poverty and lack of suitable education system are the important considerations for putting the children of this district to work. Poverty induces the children to work along with their parents either to assist them in their traditional occupations or in other engagements. Sometimes the children are forced to work so as to pay back their parent's loan and in some other cases children are put to work because they are the only support of their family. Another peculiar observation of the people of this district is that, they consider the present system of education to be tiresome and useless for their children. So their children are asked to assist them instead of attending school.

Whatsoever may be the reasons of child labour, the basic fact is that, a child is put to work at the cost of his latent talent. Moreover, the economic condition of any nation is threatened because child labour drives wages down and puts adults out of work. With this background the present study is a modest attempt to analyse some of the measures adopted by the government in general and by the National Child Labour Prevention Project in particular to rehabilitate the child workers of Bolangir district.

Hazardous Engagements

According to the provision of the Child Labour Act, various engagements where children are put to work are restricted to two distinct classifications of hazardous and non-hazardous nature. Hazardous engagements are further summerised under two categories to include hazardous occupations and hazardous processes.

Hazardous Occupations Include

1. Transport of passengers, goods and mail
2. Cylinder picking and clearing of Ash pits

3. Building operations in Railway Station premises
4. Working in catering establishments in Railway Stations and moving from one compartment to another and one platform to another inside the Railway track
5. Working in Port areas
6. Work relating to selling of crackers and fire works in temporary licence
7. Working in Automobile workshops and garages
8. Works relating to Foundries
9. Handling of toxic of flammable substances or explosives
10. Working in Mines (Underground and underwater) and Collieries
11. Working in Plastic units.

Hazardous Processes Include

1. Cigar and Bidi making
2. Carpet weaving
3. Cement manufacturing including bagging of cement
4. Cloth painting, dying and weaving including process preparatory
5. Manufacturing of Matches and Explosives
6. Mica cutting and splitting
7. Shellac manufacturing
8. Soap manufacturing

9. Wool cleaning
10. Tanning
11. Building and construction in industries
12. Incense Sticks (Agarbati) manufacturing
13. Automobile repairing and maintenance including process welding, lathe work, dinting and painting
14. Brick kiln and roof tile making
15. Cotton ginning, processing and production of hosiery goods.
16. Detergent manufacturing
17. Fabrication (Ferrous and Non-ferrous)
18. Gem cutting and polishing
19. Handling of chromites and manganese ores
20. Jute textile manufacturing and Coir making
21. Manufacturing of lime
22. Lock making
23. Manufacturing process having exposure to lead
24. Manufacturing of cement pipes, cement products and other related works
25. Manufacturing of glass, glassware including bulbs and other similar glass products
26. Manufacturing of dyes and dye stuff
27. Manufacturing, processing and handling of corrosive and toxic substances; metal cleaning and photo engraving and soldering process in electronic industries

28. Manufacturing and handling of pesticides and insecticides
29. Briquettes making
30. Manufacturing of sports goods involving exposure to synthetic materials chemicals and leathers
31. Moulding and processing of fiber glass and plastic
32. Oil expelling and refining
33. Paper making
34. Potteries and ceramic industrial activities
35. Polishing, moulding, cutting, welding and manufacturing of brass goods in all forms
36. Agricultural processing threshing and harvesting where tractors are used
37. Saw mill—all processing
38. Sericulture processing
39. Skinning, dying and processing for manufacture of leather and leather products
40. Stone breaking and stone crushing
41. Tobacco processing including manufacturing of tobacco in any form
42. Tyre making, repairing and retreading
43. Utensils making, polishing and metal buffing
44. Polythene and Silvery fiber making (All process).

Legal Protection for Children

Indian constitution has specific provisions to protect childhood against exploitation and not to employ children below the age of 14 years in any hazardous occupations.

The constitution, under the following Articles, make provision to prohibit the entry of children into hazardous engagements and regulates the services of the children in non-hazardous occupations.

Article–23 Prohibits forcible migration of child labour.

Article–24 Prohibits employment of child below the age of 14 years in any factory, mine and other hazardous occupation.

Article–39 (e) Safeguards the health and strength of the child workers and prohibits their employment in such areas where their age and strength do not suit.

Article–39 (f) Protects the childhood and youth against exploitation and moral and material abandonments.

Article–41 Secures the child's right to education and right to public assistance.

Article–45 Makes effective provisions for free and compulsory education of the children below the age of 14 years.

Article–47 Makes provisions to raise the level of nutrition and standard of living of the children.

Article–51 (c) Assures to foster respect for International Law and Treaty Obligations in the dealings of organised people with one another.

Since independence the Government's endeavour to restrict child labour into hazardous engagements have been made through different legislations relating to Factory Act. 1948; Employment of Children (Amendment) Act, 1949 and 1951; The Plantations Labour Act, 1951; Merchants Shipping Act, 1951; Mines Act, 1952; The Factories (Amendment) Act, 1954; The Merchant Shipping Act, 1958; The Motor Transport Workers Act, 1961; The Bidi and Cigar Workers (Conditions of Employment) Act, 1966; Employment of Children (Amendment) Act, 1978; Child Labour (Prohibition and Regulation) Act, 1986 etc.

Currently, a Civil Writ Petition was filed by the child labourers of Shivkasi praying for justice from the Supreme Court of India. The Honb'le Court gave the verdict on Dt. 10-12-96 with its direction to make it applicable for the entire Country. The Hon'ble Court directed the Government to conduct country-wide survey of child labour; release children from hazardous engagements and enroll them in formal and non-formal schools, initiate legal action against all offending employers by making a recovery of Rs. 20,000/- from them per child and put it in the District Child Labour Welfare Fund, make provision of Job for at least one adult member of the family of the child engaged under hazardous occupations or deposit Rs. 5000/- for each child in the Corpus Fund to aid the working children.

Role of NCLP in Bolangir

A number of Social Organisations, Non-Government Organisations and Trade Unions have also made significant contributions to pull out children from hazardous occupations "Mukti Ashram", is a transitory rehabilitation cum Vocational Training Centre for the bonded and other child workers. It organises a three-month session for 50-60 children and imparts formal education and appropriate vocational training in accordance to the child's age, interest and ability.

As a follow up action to the UNO's resolution in 1984 on the rights of children, the Government of India launched 100 National Child Labour Prevention (NCLP) Projects for the child labourers in the country during 1994-96. Orissa got a share of 16 such NCLP Projects and launched one each at Koraput, Malkangiri, Nabarangpur, Rayagada, Ganjam, Gajapati, Kalahandi, Nuapada, Bolangir, Sambalpur, Subarnapur, Jharsuguda, Anugul, Deogarh, Mayurbhanj and Balasore.

The Collector cum District Magistrate of the concerned districts became the Chairman of the project and included five district level officers and two social workers as members to form the "Society for Welfare of Child Labour" under the Society Registration Act, 1860. The Society also included the remunerative project staff namely Project Director, Field Officer, Accountant, Stenographer, Driver and Peons. The Society aimed at running special schools at different localities to provide formal education and vocational training to the working children of the concerned localities. The government plans to open 562 schools for rehabilitation of about 36750 working children in the state.

The Bolangir NCLP project was inaugurated on 31-01-96 and opened 40 special schools in conformity with the recommendations of the Block Development Officers. Keeping the intensity of child-labour in locality, schools were opened under each Block. One of each such schools were opened to function at Titilagarh NAC, Kantabanji NAC and Patnagarh NAC. Bolangir Municipality, Deogarh, Saintala, Tatilagarh, Muribahal, Turekela and Patnagarh Blocks each got to open 2 special schools whereas Bolangir, Puintala, Loisingha, Agalpur, Gudvela, Bangomunda Blocks each, has a share of 3 schools. Belpara was the only Block in the district with a share of 4 such schools. As per guidelines of the government each school is limited to a strength of fifty students. The Project of the Government aimed at rehabilitating 2000 working children of Bolangir district.

An intensive survey was made over the entire district of Bolangir to identify the working children under hazardous and non-hazardous occupations. Out of 12275 working children of Bolangir district, 2000 children, engaged under different hazardous occupations were selected for enrollment of their names in NCLP schools. These children were provided with mid-day meals and a monthly stipend of Rs. 100/- each having arrangement of depositing the same in their Savings Bank Accounts. The provision of their entertainment is also made by extending facilities for playing football, volleyball etc. Now NCLP Project of Bolangir district has successfully produced 560 adults to join the mainstream.

Conclusion

Despite adequate efforts of the Government and the Social Activities, the child workers could not be released from hazardous occupations. On one hand, it becomes easy in circumvent the law and on the other hand many models of elevation of child labour, seem quite ridiculous.

It is Easy to Circumvent the Law Because

1. The Factory Act leaves enough scope for the employers to put the children to work in such units where the employment limits from 10 to 20. The easy way to get around the legislation is to decentralise production and limit the employees as required under law so that child workers can be accommodated.

2. The Child Labour Act is too narrow to protect the children from working under hazardous conditions. According to a 'Human Rights Watch Researcher', about 92 per cent of all working children of India are not covered under the Act.

3. The problem of steady implementation of the law at the state level is prominently observed owing to disharmony in the Centre-State Relationship.

4. A Punjab Labour Department Insider, in his observation, has disclosed about the need for proper implementation of the labour laws.

Models are Defective for Elevation of Child Labour Because

1. So far Article 24, 39 and 45 of the Indian Constitution and Child Labour Act, 1986 have not ratified the Convention 138 of ILO which suggests the minimum age limit for entering into any employment should be fixed at 15 years.

2. Enrollment of children for formal education may keep them away from acquiring ancestral skill.
3. Combining formal education with employment, may not be helpful for the child in exploring his own talent.

References

1. Bhandari, J. (2000) *"Child Labour, Challenges in New Millennium"*, in Kurukshetra, Vol. 48, No. 8, May, 2000.
2. Dwarakanath, H.D. (1999) *"Child Labour Need for New Social Revolution"*, in Kurukshetra, Vol. 47, No. 6, March, 1999.
3. Husein Taha, *Child Labour in India.*
4. Mishra, L (2000) *Child Labour in India,* Oxford University Press, New Delhi.
5. Roul, H.S. (1999) *"Child Labour in Orissa: A Necessary Evil"*, in Vision, Vol. XIX, No. 1-2.
6. Weiner, M. (1991) *The Child and the State in India,* Princeton University Press.
7. Weiner, M (1996) *"Child Labour in India: Putting Compulsory Primary Education on the Political Agenda"* Economic and Political weekly, November 9-16, 1996.

9

Study of Child Labour—A Close Look

***B. Dalai**
****Dr. R.N. Misra**

Introduction

During the recent times, the Child Labour has come to be discussed widely in many circles. Voluntary organisation, the Government International organisation, Journalists and other media men have highlighted the situation of working children in the country. There is an ongoing debate about the approaches to the situation in which millions of children in the country work. While there is an agreement that the child labour should be banned in all hazardous industries, there is no one opinion about the abolition of child labour in non-hazardous industries. Children are an asset for any society. It's the responsibility of the society to nurture them through various phases of their

* Mr. Dalai is Faculty Member, Department of Commerce, B.J.B. College, Bhubaneswar (Orissa).

** Dr. Mishra is Senior Faculty Member, Department of Commerce, Science College, Hinjilcut (Orissa).

development in order to ensure for them a better quality of life. The phenomenon of millions of children working for a pillance across the globe, however is the grim reminder of the failure of the society to protect them.

What is Child Labour

Under section 2(ii) of the child labour (Prohibition and Regulation) Act 1986, the child has been defined "as child means a person who has not completed his fourteenth year of age."

The Hon'ble Supreme Court of India in their historical, judgement on child labour in writ petition (c) No.–465 of 986 M.C. Menta Vs. State of Tamil Nadu and others dated 10-12-96 has given certain directions for identification of child labour in Hazardous work and the following subsequent action to be initiated thereafter.

1. The manner in which the children working in hazardous occupations are to be withdrawn from work and rehabilitated.
2. Payment of compensation amounting to Rs. 20,000 by the offerding employer for every child employed in contravention of the provisions of the Act, for hazardous employment.
3. Giving alternation employment to an adult member of the family in the place of the child withdrawn from hazardous occupation or payment of an amount of Rs. 5,000 by the appropriate Government for each child.
4. Constitution of a fund named "Child Labour Rehabilitation cum Welfare Fund" under the chairmanship of the collector.

A working child is a child in the age group of 5 to 15 who is doing labour, either paid or unpaid and is kept working at any hour of the day within or outside the family: basically, a child who is deprived of the right of education and childhood.

What makes this definition important is that it makes it unambiguously clear that all out-of-school children are child labourers in one form or another. It does not make a distinction between children working in the so-called hazardous industries and children working as part of family labour. If child labour has to be eliminated then we have to take a holistic approach to children and not categorize them: we cannot condone that fact that some groups of children work and not others. Nevertheless, to understand the kind of work that children are subjected to in different sectors, a typology is given below.

Child Labour: Those children who are doing paid or unpaid work in factories, workshop, establishments, mines and in the service sector such as domestic labour.

Since the law prohibits the employment of children below the age of 14 in factories, mines and other hazardous employment, all such children, except those who work in the service sector or as domestic labour, can be assisted legally.

Street Children: Children living on and off the streets, such as shoe-shine boys, rag-pickers, newspaper vendors, beggars, etc. The problem of street children is somewhat different from that of child labour in factories and workshops. For one thing, most children have some sort of home to go back to in the evenings or nights, while street children are completely alone and are at the mercy of their employers. They live in the dhaba (small eating place), on the pavement, in the bus depot, or on the railway platform. They are at the mercy of criminals, drug addicts and the police. They have no permanent base and are constantly on the move. So their problem is more acute than that of children working in a factory and living at home.

Bonded Children: Children who have either been pledged by their parents for paltry sums of money or those working (mainly in rural India) to pay off the inherited debts of their fathers. Bonded children are in many ways the most difficult to assist because they are inaccessible. In the dhaba owner has bought them, they cannot escape. If the middle-class house wife has paid for them, they cannot run away. If the landlord in the village owns them, they will spend their life in servitude till they get married, and can in turn sell their children.

Working Children: Children who are working as part of family labour in agriculture and in home-based work. If children are working 12-14 hours a day along with their parents at the cost of their education, their situation is similar to that of children working for other employers. In fact children, particularly girls, are expected to take on work burdens by parents in complete disproportion to their strength and abilities.

Hazardous

As per part 'A' and 'B' of the schedule to the child labour (Prohibition and Regulation) Act, 1986 child labour has been prohibited to work in certain hazardous and occupation.

PART 'A'—HAZARDOUS

1. Transport of passengers, goods or mails by railways
2. Cylinder packing, clearing of as ashpit a building operation in the railways premise
3. Work in a catering establishment at a railway station. The movement of a vendor of any other employee of the establishment from one platform to another of into or out of a moving train. Work relating to the construction of a railway station or

with any other work where such work is done in close proximity for between the railway lines

4. A port authority within the limits of any port

5. Work relating to selling of crackers and fine works in shops with temporary licences

6. Abattoirs/slaughter house.

PART 'B'—OCCUPATION

1. Beedi making
2. Carpet weaving
3. Cement manufacture including of bagging of cement
4. Cloth printing, dyeing and weaving
5. Manufacturing of matches
6. Mica cutting and splitting
7. Shell manufacture
8. Soap manufacture
9. Tanning
10. Building and construction industry
11. Wool clearing
12. Hazardous process as defined in section 2 (cb) and dangerous operations as notified in rules made under Sec. 87 of the Factories Act, 1948 (63 to 1948).

The list of industries which are involving in hazardous process are given below.

1. *Farrows Metallurgical Industries:* Integrated Iron and Steel, Ferrow alloys, special steels

2. *Coal (including coke) Industries:* Coal lignite coke etc., Full Gases (including coal, gas, producer Gas.)

3. Power generating Industries

4. *Fertilizer Industries;* Nitrogenous, Phosphatic, mixed

5. *Petroleum Industries:* Oil Refining, Lubricating oils and greases

6. *Drugs and Pharmaceutical Industries:* Narcotics, drugs.

Child labour working in hazardous occupations are mostly found in the organised sector in areas, where people are not aware of their right, their poverty, illiteracy, lack of awareness and at times large family size making them easy prey for such exploitation. However it is to be noted that those in organised sectors are greatly organised perpetuate this exploitation. The most important starting point in identifying child labour is the survey. The survey should be limited only to the working children (currently employed and also employed any time during past) in hazardous work.

Causes and Consequences of Child Labour

Does child labour cause poverty or is it poverty that causes labour? This has been the raging debate in India for the last ten years. It is the contention of this author that child labour is the cause of poverty. If poverty has to be eradicated, there has to be a frontal attack on child labour. Child labour is the result of the exploitation of the weak and the vulnerable and it is always the poorest sections of society who are most vulnerable to this exploitation. When children start working at a young age they remain illiterate, unskilled and unable to demand their rights for equal wages and better conditions of work. Working long hours, they burn themselves out and their health is severely impaired. As adults, in situations like these, they are often heavily in debt. The circumstances of unemployment—if not un-employability—combined with their inferior position in the hierarchies of caste and class, predispose them to putting their own children to work. And so the downward spiral of exploitation and poverty is perpetuated. Forced at an early age to accept poor working conditions, long hours of work and less than minimum wages, the poor find themselves, not surprisingly, in a state of 'false consciousness'—believing. That their exploiters are their benefactors. Child labour therefore becomes acceptable even to those most affected by it.

So all pervasive is the belief that without poverty eradication child labour cannot be eliminated, that we have taken this reasoning as irrefutable. The questions that are most often asked are: What will happen to the families of these children if child labour is eradicated? How will poor families survive without the additional income of the children? It is seldom taken into account that children's earnings are pathetically meagre, and that it is precisely because of the vast numbers of children in the work-force in all sectors of the economy that adult wages are depressed. In most cases, the child is used by parents as an asset to mortgage, when all other assets disappear.

SOME EXAMPLES ON HAZARDOUS OCCUPATION

The Case of Firozabad

Almost 50,000 children in the age range of 10-14 years are employed at present in the glass factories of Firozabad. The temperatures in the furnaces in the glass bangle and glass blowing industry range from 700ºC to 1400ºC. Children carry iron rods to the tank furnaces and draw out molten glass. They run with this to the glass blower or bangle maker. Accidents are very common. It takes only 3 to 4 years to damage young lungs in the dangerously polluted atmosphere of the glass factories.

State Industry of Mandsaur, Madhya Pradesh

The State Industry of Mandsaur employs thousands of children. They cut plates of state into small pieces with electrically operated saws, a process which emits dense clouds of a fine, light dust. This leads to solicosis, a disease that causes fibrous changes in the lungs which are gradually eaten away. Patients suffer respiratory trouble, begin to spit blood and die a painful death. Children at the age of 12 and even less are forced into this fatally hazardous work to support their dying parents, brothers and sisters, only to find, soon enough, that they will die too.

Match Industry of Sivakasi, Tamil Nadu

Children who work in the boiler rooms mixing chemicals are exposed to toxic fumes, suffer high degrees of intense heat and run the risk of being badly injured by fire accidents. Children who stamp frames on the metal sheet, too suffer heat, toxic fumes and excessive strain on the arms and shoulders as they have to remove and place the heavy frames with great rapidity. Delay could cause the entire frame to go up in flames causing instant death.

These are some extreme examples of what happens when children work in factories and workshops. But there are many more examples: from the lock industry of Aligarh and the brassware industry of Moradabad in Uttar Pradesh, and the balloon factories in Dahanu, Maharashtra, to name only a few.

Child Labour Position of Orissa

According to 1981 census, child labour constitute about 6 per cent of the total work-force in the state of Orissa and child labour engaged in various sectors are detailed below.

The Table—9.1 indicates that the major level of employment of child labour is in the agrarian sector. Out of

Table—9.1 Child Labour Position in Various Sectors

Sl. No.	Name of the Sector	Male child	Female child	Total
1.	Cultivators	151641	23980	175621
2.	Agriculture labourers	168871	77967	246838
3.	Livestock, forestry and fishing etc.	26771	5078	31849
4.	Mining and quarrying	655	884	1549
5.	Manufacturing processing servicing and repairing			
	(a) Household work	8078	6972	15050
	(b) Other than household	7860	2608	10468
6.	Construction work	859	1268	2127
7.	Trade and Commerce	8407	1369	9776
8.	Transport, storage and communication	682	92	774
9.	Other services	13992	7302	21295
	Total	**387827**	**127520**	**515347**

5.15 lakh of child labour in the state. 4.2 lakh of child labour i.e. 82 per cent below to this agrarian sector. Remaining 18 per cent of child labour is distributed in other industry including mining. Employment of child labour is very much negligible in the transport and communication. Percentage of employment of child labour is on higher side in livestock, farms and fishery and 96.86 per cent of the total child labour are engaged in the rural sector and the remaining 5.14 per cent in the urban sector. Coming to distributions of child work accrue to 75.25 per cent belong to male child labour and 24.75 per cent to female child labour. Employment of female child workers were 23.37 per cent in the rural sector and 1.38 per cent in the urban sector. Similarly 71.74 per cent of the male child worker were employed in the rural sector and 3.76 per cent in the urban sector. Employment of male child workers was predominant is both the urban and rural sectors as compared to the female child labour section in state-wise distribution of child worker (0-14) age group. August 1971 to 1981 and 1992 constant are explained in Table—9.2.

Suggestion

To achieve the objective of elimination of child labour, it has become imperative that appropriate emphasis must be placed on implementation of all the main ingredients of the National Child Labour Policy of 1987 through well developed schemes and programmes in an integrated manner. To achieve this following suggestions and recommendations are made for deliberation and action.

1. It is necessary to carry out comprehensive door-to-door surveys to identify child labour and build up a socio-economic profile of affected families under the supervision of the State Government.

2. With data from these surveys it is possible to draw up a comprehensive long-term plan 1995-2000 (A.D.) which may then be divided into annual plan for each year.

Table—9.2 State-wise Distribution of Child Workers (0-14) Age Group According to 1971, 1981 and 1991 Census.

Sl. No.	State/Union Territories	*Child workers in the age 0–14 (Millions)*				
		1971	*1981*	*1991*		
				Main child workers	*Marginal child workers*	*Total child workers*
1	2	3	4	5	6	7
1.	Andhra Pradesh	1,627,492	1,951,312	1,537,293	124,647	1,661,940
2.	Assam	239,349		259,953	67,645	327,598
3.	Bihar	1,059,359	1,101,764	795,444	146,801	942,245
4.	Gujarat	518,061	616,913	373,027	150,558	523,585
5.	Haryana	137,826	194,189	89,030	20,661	109,691
6.	Himachal Pradesh	71,384	99,624	30,771	25,667	56,438
7.	Jammu and Kashmir	70,489	258,437	0		
8.	Karnataka	808,719	1,131,530	818,159	158,088	976,247

(Contd...)

Table—9.2 (Contd...)

1	2	3	4	5	6	7
9.	Kerala	111,801	92,854	28,590	6,210	34,800
10.	Madhya Pradesh	1,112,319	1,698,597	997,940	354,623	1,352,563
11.	Maharashtra	988,357	1,557,756	805,847	262,571	1,068,418
12.	Manipur	16,380	20,217	13,478	3,015	16,493
13.	Meghalaya	30,440	44,916	30,730	3,903	34,633
14.	Nagaland	13,726	16,235	16,106	370	16,476
15.	Orissa	492,477	702,293	325,250	127,144	452,394
16.	Punjab	232,774	216,939	132,414	10,454	142,868
17.	Rajasthan	587,389	819,605	490,522	283,677	774,199
18.	Sikkim	15,661	8,561	5,254	344	5,598
19.	Tamil Nadu	713,305	975,055	523,125	55,764	578,889
20.	Tripura	17,490	24,204	13,506	2,972	16,478
21.	Uttar Pradesh	1,326,726	1,434,675	1,145,087	264,999	1,410,086

(Contd...)

1	2	3	4	5	6	7
22.	West Bengal	511,443	605,263	593,387	118,304	711,691
23.	Andaman and Nikobar Islands	572	1,309	758	507	1,265
24.	Arunachal Pradesh	17,925	17,950	11,632	763	12,395
25.	Chandigarh	1,086	1,986	1,839	31	1,870
26.	Dadra and Nagar Haveli	3,102	3,615	2,677	1,739	4,416
27.	Delhi	17,120	25,717	26,670	681	27,351
28.	Daman and Diu	7,391	9,378	741	200	941
29.	Goa	3,938	718	4,656		
30.	Lakshadweep	97	56	17	17	34
31.	Mizoram		6,314	6,391	10,020	16,411
32.	Pondichery	3,725	3,606	2,565	115	2,680
	Total	**10,753,985**	**13,640,870**	**9,082,141**	**2,203,208**	**11,285,349**

Source : Report on National Seminar on Implementation of National Child Labour Project, National Reso Centre on Child Labour, V.V. Giri National Labour Institute, NOIDA, 1996 p. 186-188.

3. The action plan must include appropriate schemes and programmes on all the three ingredients of the N.C.L. policy.

4. Programmes and schemes should also be directed and preventing potential child labour from becoming working children.

References

1. *Souvenir, Swechhasebi, Samanwoya Samiti,* Orissa, Bhubaneswar. 25th February, 1996.

2. Khatel, K.K. et. al. *Working Children in India* Banoda Operation Research Group, 1983.

3. Burra Neera, *Born of Work, Child Labour in India*—Oxford University Press, 1995.

4. Mitra Nirmal, *Starved Children of Mandsaur.* Sunday June, 15.01.1986.

5. Vishwapriya 1, Lycngar *"Where Children Labour and Fathers Despair".* Indian Express, February 16, 1986.

6. Shukla Sudhindra *"Little Oves Meandering in the Dark"* National Herald, March 25, 1984.

7. Prembhai Report to the Supreme Court Regarding *Child Weavers of Mirzapur.* Bhadohi Varanasi Mirzapur Banwasi Eva, Ashram, 1984 (unpublished).

8. National Resources Centre on Child Labour.

9. State Labour Institute Kharavel Nagar, Bhubaneswar.

10

Child Labour: Causes, Consequences and Cure

***Mrs. Babilata Shroff**

Man has to pass through many stages of life out of which childhood is most important because it is the formative period of life. It is also the first conscious stage of life. Human character takes its shape in childhood because at this stage the mind is soft and receptive. Every parents and the society wants its children to grow into good and responsible citizens. This is possible when the children are given nutritious, food, proper education, good shelter, better environment, constructive instruction, affection and direction as well as proper guidance. Lack of these facilities puts the lifes of youngsters in jeopardy. Child labour is an example of this, which is a form of exploitation due to lack of protection; both from the family and the society. Child labour is economically unsound, psychologically disastrous, physically dangerous and ethically a matter of great concern.

* Lecturer in Economics, D.A.V. College, Titlagarh, District Bolangir (Orissa)

The question of child labour has entered the public consciousness with some persistence and the debate on this subject was initiated mainly by the press and media, social activities and academicians when the Govt. announced its intention in 1985 to introduce fresh legislations to deal with the phenomenon of child labour.

Who is a Child Labour?

There is a diversity among researchers in defining child labour and it is due to differences in social perceptions.

Homer Folks, Chairman of the United States Child Labour Committee defined child labour "as any work done by children, that interferes with their full physical and mental development, their opportunities for a desirable minimum of education or their needed recreation."

V.V. Giri, Late President of India delineated two different senses of child labour, firstly as an economic practice through which a child is an economic unit of the family through earning; secondly, as the exposure of the child to social hazards, the dangers of physical labour and concurrently, the denial of the opportunities of development.

Franscis Blanchard, the Director General of the ILO states "child labour can be conceived to include children under the age of 15 years in work or employment with the aim of earning a livelihood for themselves or for their families."

The population below the age of 15 years are treated as children. A child labour is a working child who is employed in a gainful occupation and in the process of work may be exposed to injurious work and also may be deprived of developmental opportunities. According to the International Bureau of Statistics Report of 1980 nearly 95 per cent of children in the age group of 10-15 years of the world help their family at different times as unpaid workers. From one angle the unpaid child family workers should not be considered as child labour. Because a family is an economic unit where all the members are responsible for maintaining family and in the process contribute towards the upkeep of the whole family; a child may be required to work in the house. On the other hand, the meaning of child labour will be narrow if we do not consider the causes of children either self-employed or employed in the household/family occupations and in the process contribute towards the upkeep of the whole family, a child may be required to work in the house. On the other hand, the meaning of child labour will be narrow if we do not consider the causes of children either self-employed or employed in the household/family occupations either as full-time or part-time workers (opportunity cost of employment should be calculated). In India, most of the girls are not allowed to go outside the native place and work as unpaid family workers being deprived of education another things required for their growth and development. Hence a broader definition of child labour should include that segment of child population which participate in paid and unpaid work.

International Labour Organisation (ILO) defined child labour as "work regularly done by the children under the age of 15 with very limited exceptions." It distinguished "child work" and "child labour defining former as "spending few hours a day of on tasks which are not enormous—can raise child's self esteem, teach a trade for the future help the family" and the later as "long hours of hard slog, detrimental to a child's schooling and damaging to his or her emotional, physical and psychological development."

The Encyclopaedia of Social Sciences (1959) defines child labour as "when the business of wage earnings or of participation in self or family support conflicts directly or indirectly with the business of growth and education the result is child labour.

Magnitude of Child Labour

Child labour is a global phenomenon. ILO in 1996 estimated 250 million child labourers economically active all over the world—atleast 120 million of them were on full-time basis while the others were combing their work with schooling. 50 to 60 million of them work in hazardous occupations. In Malaysia, they are forced to work in rubber plantation being exposed to insect and snake bites, in Tanzania in coffee gardens inhaling poisonous pesticides, in Portugal, children work in hazardous and exploitative construction industries. Thousands of Pakistani children are engaged in the hazardous leather industry like soccer balls manufacturing units. Even in development countries like USA children of most of immigrants or ethnic-minority families work in agriculture exposing themselves to pesticides spray daily. The urban centres of Latin America have the largest population of street children in the world. Regionally, it is highest for Africa (approximately 41%) followed by Asia (22%) and Latin America (13%). But in absolute terms most child workers (61%) of the world's total are in Asia, excluding Japan, as compared to 32 per cent in Africa and 7 per cent in Latin America. It is also totally absent in USSR and Australia. Major proportion of child workers in the world are present in the developing countries. In Asian countries, economically active children are highly prevalent in Nepal followed by Bangladesh. Table—10.1 shows economically active children in some of the neighbouring countries of India.

According to the 1991 census child workers the country are 11.28 millions whereas it was 13.5 millions in 1981 and 10.7 millions in 1971. The 1991 census also shows that there is a continuous decline in the proportion of child labour to child population (12.7% in 1961, 7.1% in 1971, 6.1% in 1981, and 5.9% in 1991). The National Institute of Occupational Health estimated (based on census data) that child participation in hazardous industries increased more than 200 per cent between 1961 to 1981 while it is evident from the survey results of 43rd and 50th round of NSSO study that the percentage of child labour declined from 4.1 per cent in 1987–88 to 3 per cent in 1993-94.

Table—10.1 Estimated of Economically Active Children in Some of the Neighbouring Countries of India in 1995 (Percentage of Total Children in 10 to 14 Years).

Countries	*Economically Active Children*
Bangladesh	30.1
China	11.6
India	14.4
Pakistan	17.4
Indonesia	09.6
Japan	00.0
Nepal	45.2
Thailand	16.1

Source : ILO.

According to the Ministry of Labour, Annual Report, 1996–97 Andhra Pradesh ranks first i.e., 11.2 per cent (1.66 million) of total child labour in the country followed by Karnataka (8.7%). Kerla is at the bottom of the list. Orissa occupies 3rd position with 8.31 lakhs child workers in 1994. 2.8 lakhs child labourers were added to the work force between 1981 and 1994. Orissa accounts for 9.13 per cent of the country's female child labour and 5.36 per cent of the male child workers. 87 per cent of the total identified child labourers are from South-West Orissa. Bidi making, brick making, rice mills, stone crushing blacksmith, etc. absorbs and overwhelming 66 per cent of total child labour under hazardous occupations. Uniquely, Sambalpur district has the highest number of boys (1248) and girls (3563) child labour among all the districts under hazardous occupations. The NCLP in 1995 has identified 3878 child labourers (2441 male and 1347 female) in Berhampur city, the cultural and commercial capital of southern Orissa. In Orissa the percentage of child workers was 4.58 per cent in 1971. 5.15 per cent during 1981 and reduced marginally to 4.01 per cent during 1991. The Labour Statistics of Orissa 1997 reveals that 2,15,222 (56.50% male and 43.50% female) children and engaged in 1,74,811 establishments/work sites.

District-wise distribution of child workers in the State shows that Nawarangpur (tribal dominated and backward) is at the top of the list with 15.19 per cent of child labour followed by Mayurbhanj (10.11%), Kalahandi (6.83%) and Koraput (6.30%). It is very low for the advanced districts like Jagatsinghpur (0.19%) and Sundergarh (0.40%). Facilities available for education, tribal population, availability of agricultural land, literacy rate, etc. are responsible for the differences in the magnitude of the child labour among countries, states and districts.

The sector-wise distribution of child labour shows a high concentration in the unorganised sectors and mostly in rural areas. A major portion of child workers are engaged in the primary sector where more children work in the agricultural activities.

Some children work as full-time and some as part time paid/unpaid workers sometimes in villages and urban slums children go to school but in off hours are engaged in part-time jobs like domestic servants, street-traders, rag-pickers, newspaper-setters etc.

Why Child Labour Exists

In an International seminar on the Health of Minors, Dr. B.L. Bataur told that one child in every four children is working in India out of necessity. It is true for the child workers, who irrespective of the area to which they belong—whether it is developed or underdeveloped, and village, semi-urban or urban area. Orissa Labour Directorate observes that 74 per cent of total child labours are forced to work due to abject poverty. Normally children work as paid and unpaid workers due to *Economic, Social, Psychological, and Environmental* factors (there may be an overlapping among these factors).

Economic Factors: Very often children are compelled to work due to the economic benefits which they bestow upon their parents or family members. Economic benefits are the benefits which the parents and or other members of the family receive or expect to receive from their children in the form of regular or irregular assistance in the shape of money, food and housing, support in old age and help or assistance in the house, firm or in business. Some think the children's contribution in the family income is positive because the amount of money or the labour they contribute exceeds that which is spent of on them. Thus, those who have few resources respond to adversity not by decreasing their family size but by increasing it.

The question of economic benefits from children is associated with several factors like poverty, burden of unproductive consumers, indebtedness, run away population growth resulting in large family size, migration, disturbances in the traditional occupations status maintenance in the materialistic society etc. According to the Planning Commission's estimates Expert Group Methodology percentage of population below the poverty line in 1994-95 is 39.6 per cent (40.7% for rural and 36.6% for urban areas). This percentage is still higher for Orissa (48.3%). Orissa is a store house of cheap labourers since a large number of families are below poverty line. As more than one-third areas of the States are scheduled areas and most of agricultural lands have no irrigation facilities (67%) and 38.26 per cent of the population consists of scheduled tribes, who still believe in their traditional system of living, showing their resistance towards education and modernisation; the State makes very slow progress in comparison to the advanced states of the country. The dependency ratio for Orissa is 0.950 and 0.801

in rural and urban families respectively. Other things being equal, inclusion of children into employment reduces this ratio.

The growth of population resulting into large family size (mainly among the low income group) aggravates the problem along with poverty. The job opportunities do not increase at the same rate at which the population increases. This leaves many adult members unemployed. Because of this children are completed to go for work and share the economic burden of the family, instead of availing education, recreation etc.

The child labourers who are found in urban areas are mostly the migrant children, living in the slums or in the sheds of their masters. Widespread poverty and destitution of landless rural population lie at the root of the problem. They mainly work in the shops and commercial establishments, construction works, domestic sectors or in self-employment as rickshaw-pullers, shoe-shinner, street-traders, rag-pickers etc. Sometimes the situation raised due to the disturbances in their traditional occupations resulted by the natural calamities. Due to non-availability of work in the rural areas particularly in the hill areas and drought areas of Orissa, people go outside the state to work in textile mills, coal mines, construction projects, or as hotel boys as migrants workman. Boys of 12 to 15 years of age are also seen migrated with other family members and face the exploitation of the Sardars, Thikadars and Contractors.

Sometimes children go to work with their parents as a helping hand and also work independently to find a place of job for future. Otherwise, the migrant parents depute the little hands with the household/traditional/family occupations during their absence.

According to the report of Indian Social Institute on Child Labour (1986) there are 3,50,000 bonded labourers in the State out of which children constitute 20.4 per cent. The poor landless agricultural labourers and backward people incur loans from the landlords or moneylenders for unproductive purposes like marriages, funerals, etc. They engage themselves and all their family members including children to repay the loan. This system continuous for generations as the loan is not repaid due to high rate of interest and exploitative attitude of the landlord towards the innocent, ignorant and illiterate people.

Economic frustration with a feeling of deprivation of objectives and the tendency among the low income groups to maintain status in the materialistic society where all the decisions are in favour of the elite class sometime gives birth to child labour.

We, the so called literate, advanced and modern citizens prefer children for our domestic sector, construction projects, etc. because it is easy to exploit them and derive the surplus value. As they are children with a weak bargaining power, we take advantage by deriving surplus value in terms of wage paid, works done and working hours.

Social Factors

The orphans without well-wishers are compelled to work to maintain their own lives. In many cases, among the low income groups children of diseased, gambler or drug-addicted parents go for works to maintain themselves and their families.

Sometimes, neglected children with step-fathers (common in western countries but countable in our society) or step mothers are deprived of love, affection and things required for the healthy growth. In this situation also some of them work as child workers.

Very often in our society a girl child is a victim of the genders bias. To provide comfort to the male children, the illiterate parents send their daughters to work. The most important factor responsible are ignorance and illiteracy.

(Literacy rate is 36% in India and 31% for Orissa and the school drop out rate is 64.86% for Orissa).

Robert K. Morten an American sociologist in his book Social Structure and Anomie pointed out that economic frustration sometimes results into drug-trafficing among boys and prostitution among girls. Alber Cohen's, delinquent Sub-culture theory also points out that the delinquent children develop their own means and goals which are against the main values.

Psychological Factors

Among the psychological factors 'Emotion' among children is also responsible for the emergence of child labour. Here the influence of media should not be ignored. Though, many low income earners do not have Televisions, they enjoy it outside the house. The influence of some programmes sometimes fall on them. Ex—a hero in his childhood wandering round the streets or working as a child labour becoming a powerful person (a great business man/politician/ film actor) leaves an image on some children. Out of emotion, they work as child labourers. (Some children of well-to-do families also leave house) sometimes also children involve themselves in the unwanted friend circle or television programmes and neglect their studies. When punished or scolded bitterly by the elders some of them leaves home and work as child workers. Out of the frustrations of being deprived of the means (discussed earlier) some children work as child labour.

Sometimes illusion among children covert them into child workers, while at home they look at the ice-creamwallas, thelawallas, hotels or restaurants feel that the people working there must be enjoying a lot of ice-creams, sweets, samosas etc. and enjoying the company of many people. As they are the inmatures, cannot see the things happening behind the screen" How the hotel boys eat the left outs", "How the master behaves them", etc.

Some children prefer to work as the domestic servants in the houses of government or semi-government employees. They have an illusion that if they enter as domestic servants first, later on there is chance of being employed in their offices.

Environmental Factors

Sometimes the environment in which the child grows is also responsible for this. The effects of urbanisation and industrialisation has not changed the attitude, class system and casteism among the people. It is found that with development the rich are becoming more richer and poor remaining at the same place. On the other hand, child labour has changed radically due to industrialisation by providing industry's comparative advantage in international markets.

Free education and compulsory education for all who are below 14 years of age are yet to be successful in all the areas of the State. The school drop out rate at the lower primary, upper primary and middle school levels are 63.5 per cent, 77.7 per cent and 84.1 per cent respectively. After 53 years of independence also the powerful, privileged and elite classes of people are exploiting the innocent, ignorant and illiterate masses. They seat in conferences, tables, and seminars to discuss about the well-being of the exploited masses but never want to put into practice. They have a fear of losing power. Above all, when a child finds many like him are working and earning his surrounding, he also feels himself eligible and fit for work.

Evil Consequences of Child Labour

The phenomenon of child labour is deep-rooted in socio-economic stratification, restricted job opportunities and prevailing poverty situation of rural India. It is a social malady and one of the greatest social malaise which vibrates towards the under development of the economy without supporting qualitative population growth.

Most of the families living below poverty line suffer from alienation, illiteracy, poverty, malnutrition, inferiority, social evils and pessimism. The traditional values and aptitude in respect to the child among these groups have kept them at a disadvantaged position in the society. The parents from these deprived groups do not only send their children to work but also deprived them of numerous opportunities required for a healthy social living. These children reveals several characters like frustration, aggression, delinquency, inferiority complex, alienation, lack of proper motivation and identification with the school community. They are, responsible for the highest educational wastage in India and also national talent. It is a recognised fact that all the work they do are not harmful to them. But their participation in work force at a very tender age tells upon their full physical development and deprives them of educational opportunities.

70 per cent of the child workers and paid only a fraction of wage of the adults who are doing the same work. They are susceptible to coercion; the employers make them to work for long hours and subject them to various kinds of harassments and abuses.

The phenomenon of child labour is reflected in the higher incidence of dropouts in rural schools and higher fertility among couples in low income homes in rural areas. Because couples who want children for economic benefits tend to have higher fertility in comparison with these who want children primarily for religious, social or emotional reasons.

Economic freedom at an early age, particularly in case of the boys frequently encourage them to develop bad habits such as gambling, excessive drinking of country-liquor, bidi-smoking, frequent visit to movies and other cheap sources of urban entertainment. The attraction towards an urban life style results in extravagant expenditure. The wage, rather than going to the family's income pool is used by himself. This leads to conflict and tension in the family. Sometimes these extravagant expenditures encouraged delinquent activities like pick-pocket, stealing, etc.

When the question of migrant child workers arise their problems are many and complex. They range from the problems of practical and financial nature to problems of socialisation, family dis-organisation, health, recreation, education and alienation, problems vary from urban to rural setting as well as from occupation to occupation.

In the domestic front the number of activities the children perform are cleaning, cooking, washing clothes, taking care of children, watering the plants etc. When a single pie is lost in the house she/he is the first person to be shocked. But in an agrarian society they go beyond these to the maintenance of livestock, protection crops from birds and animals, weeding, etc. Their works create situation for a dark future for them and the only choice left upon them is to inherit the traditional family occupation and a miserable life. The agricultural sector, children have to work in the scorching heat of summer (cause headache and sun burns), biting cold of winter (develops fissures in hands and feat), penetrating dust storm and/or pouring waters. They are also exposed to the chemical fertilisers and pesticides on the one hand and poisonous snakes and scorpions on the other.

The self-employed children very often face the wrath of the police, municipal employees, adults employed in the same occupation, drunkards and anti-social elements. In bidi-industries, children are exposed to tobacco fuels throughout the day, which leads to tuberculosis and asthma. Continuous cold, backache, body-ache, gas trouble rheumatic complaints are common as the workers have to sit in the over-crowded places lacking ventilation.

The most dangerous, demanding and destructive of self-worth is the job of scarp-collectors or rag-pickers. They scrounge dusbins and garbage dumps in search of paper, rags scarp of tin, iron, glass pieces and even food that others have thought fit to be thrown away. Sometimes they are seen fighting with stray dogs for a piece of mild bread.

In construction works and projects children use to carry the bricks, bolders, rods, cement bags etc. They also water the constructed house/building either standing in the broken walls, old ladders or incomplete house itself. These involve risk. Getting little sleep and being busy in their tasks against the red eyes of the master, their eyes itch and burn. Most of the child workers found in the domestic sector, construction works, agricultural activities, hotels, thelas, scarp collection etc. in the towns like Bhubaneswar, Sambalpur, Berhampur, or semi-urban area like, Titilagarh, villages like, Bhatipara and Shatighat almost all have cuts/wounds, cold, frequent fever body aches etc. are common problems.

We have also evidences of children working in match and fire work industries at Shivakasi in Tamil Nadu, stone quarries and slate industries in Kerala, fish freezing and processing centres in Kerala, handloom industries in Trivandrum (Kerala), Tiripur and Bhiwandi (Maharashtra) bidi industries in Tiruchirrapalli (Tamil Nadu) and Tirichur (Kerala), lock industries in Aligarh (U.P.) handicraft industries in Jammu and Kashmir, carpet weaving in Kashmir, Varanasi, Bhadohi and Mirzapur, glass industries in Ferozabad (U.P.), Jem polishing in Jaipur (Rajasthan), coir industries in Kerala, pottery in Khurja (U.P.), brassware in Moradabad (U.P.) etc. These are the hazardous occupation in which children are used. In the glass bangle and glass glowing industries, children work close to the furnace where the temperature ranges from 700 degree centigrade to 1800 degree centigrade. They work with cyanide and silica. Here tuberculosis is widespread and most of the workers are unable to work after they reach 35 years.

The carpet industries most of the children work on the looms located in dingy and dark sheds, which lacks proper ventilation and sitting capacity. Tuberculosis and asthma are common diseases developed by them. They also suffer from bodyaches, joint and finger pains, redness of eyes and feeling of weakness. Lack of exercise and constant sitting on the posture results into loss of appetite. A bend posture adversely affects and reproductive capacity of the female children. Children in match and fire works industries at Shivakasi handle dangerous and poisonous chemicals such as potassium chlorate, phosphorous and zinc oxide. They develop skin and eye diseases, and occasional explosions in the factory prove fatal to them. In stone quarries and slate industries children inhale silicon dust, which reduces their oxygen absorption capacity and create respiratory problems. In fish pealing centres, the work starts after the arrival of fish. So children have to work continuously from evening till the work completes.

In the lock industries and metal industries the chemical fuels affect the respiratory system and the hot fumes affect vision. The hazardous in the brassware industries are inhaling of metal dust leading to tuberculosis.

Lack of education and formal training as well as early employment badly affect the physical health. Sometimes life span and degenerates mental health and reduces the earning capacity at a later age. Though the child labour supplements the family income to some extent, it reduces the income generation by lowering the wage rate and escalating the adult unemployment and under-employment.

Child Labour and International Agencies

There are a number of International Agencies like UNO, ILO etc. which show serious concern and make provisions for child right and child labour elimination, child right got global recognition in 1990. Stockholm conference in 1996 and

OSLO conference in 1997 on child right and child labour reaffirmed this global issue.

The moralists of the West clamor for abandon or at least strict and uniform code of conduct across countries for employment of child labour. Poor enforcement of labour standard in developing countries make exportable good keepers due to cheap labour employment such as child labour. From ethical point of view (it may be for selfish reasons) WTO exerts pressure to maintain uniform labour standards for the protection of workers like ban on child labour.

Existing Legislative Measures

Children were used to be sold as slaves for doing low and dishonourable works in ancient India. Kautilya, by law, prohibited the sale of children below eight years of age *(Kautilya, Arthashastras),* Manu has also pointed out this in *Manusamhita.* In the welfare state like India the state has a responsibility towards the downtrodden little citizens. To prevent and protect children from child labour the first law as enacted in 1881 and since then several protective measures were enforced through new laws from time to time. Article 15 (3), Article 24, Article 39 (e) of Articles 39 (f) and Article 45 of the constitution of India—all state for the healthy development of children and free and compulsory education for all children until they complete the age of 14 years.

Besides the constitutional provisions, employment of children is regulated by the Factories Act. 1948 Mines Act. 1952 Motor Transport Act. 1951 Motor Transport Act. Plantation Labour Act. 1951, Merchant Shipping Act 1958. Apprenticeship Act. Bidi and Cigarettes Act 1956 and Shops and Commercial Establishments Act 1952.

Again, the child labour (Prohibition and Regulation) Act 1986, is a comprehensive law which prohibits employment of children in hazard occupations and processes which are harmful for the physical and mental growth of the children. It also regulates the working conditions such as restricting working hour, banning night work, etc. in other employments where children work. Here, it is mentioned clearly that those who employ children in the occupations and processes in which their employment is prohibited are liable to be punished with imprisonment for a term of not less than 3 months but may extend to 1 year. Any person, police officer or an inspector can file a case against any employer for an offence under this act in any court of competent jurisdiction. A National Advisory Body by the labour department can suggest inclusion of other occupations hazardous, if they find.

In spite of improved legislations like implementation of Child Labour Act 1986 and National Policy on Labour and other action programmes for welfare of child labourers the incidence of child labour in the country has not been brought down to a significant extent.

As per the 1993-94 report of the State Education Department the drop out rates in classes 1 to 5 are 47 per cent and classes 1 to 8 are 62 per cent National sample survey conducted in September 1994 by the National Council of Applied Economic Research Reports that the percentage of non-enrolled children is higher. To increase enrollment, check the school drop out, promote and universalise primary education, the government has introduced the Mid-day Meal Programme since 15th August, 1995. In Tamil Nadu it is more successful but in Orissa where poverty is widespread the struggle for existence supercedes peoples attitude towards education. Hence majority of poor people prefer to spend children for work without being attracted by a lunch in the school. The efforts made to break the vicious circle of illiteracy is yet to be successful.

The NCLP is established and has undertaken a major activity like the establishment of special schools to provide non-formal education, vocational training, supplementary nutrition, free books stationaries, uniforms etc. to children withdrawn from employment. Rs. 100/- is also provided by opening a bank account in their names. Under the project based action plan of the policy, 12 NCLPs were started in Andhra Pradesh, Bihar, M.P., Maharashtra, Orissa, Rajasthan, Tamil Nadu and U.P. By 1997, 76 child labour project under the NCLP (National Child Labour Project) Schemes have been sanctioned for covering 1.5 lakhs children.

Besides all these efforts we find child workers in our surroundings.

Need of the Hour

Planning and developing an appropriate strategy for elimination of child labour needs a thorough understanding of different dimensions of the problem and issues relating to rehabilitation of child labourers.

To tackle the problem of child labour long-term measures like creation on conditions by providing a proper climate and social security and package of short-term measures including the regulation of hours or work, weekly holidays, health, recreation, safety, welfare, etc. are necessary.

As the problem of child labour is interwoven with the basic survival issues of their families, its elimination cannot be thought of without considering a comprehensive welfare measures for their families as a whole. It should be a package deal involving the provision of employment opportunities available to the parents, encouragement towards a small family size along with provision of direct benefits of the child labourers. Such welfare measures can be integrated in various national development programmes as well as action programmes implemented by the voluntary organisation.

Simply after thinking over the poverty eradication and income generation programmes for the parents, the problems may not be solved. The parents must be made aware of the negative consequences of child labour and the benefits of free education as well as other provision of the government. To make the parents aware we must encourage adult education. If, at all, children are employed, they must be aware of the minimum wages act and the exploitations made by the employers. The media, social workers, students and village/ slum school teachers can undertake this awareness programme.

The employers should be made aware of the child labour (Prohibition and Regulation) Act, Minimum Wages Act, etc., and also regarding working hours, rest interval, type of works, etc., moral, social and legal consciousness should be generated amongst the employers through media, trade unions and voluntary organisations.

Awareness generation among government officials could be done by updating government officials of the latest developments such as different Acts and Policies regarding wages, age at employment, working hours, etc. Special workshop for them on problems concern could change their overall attitude towards the downtrodden. The media and the research organisations can play an important role here.

Another most important group we should be made aware of are of the general public regarding the evil effects of child labour and legal measures adopted by the government regarding child labour. Public can help working children by protecting them against the anti-social elements and exploitation by the employers. According to the child labour Act, 1986, and body can lodge a complaint against the employers. This awareness could be created by mass media, strict plays in the villages and complain in fairs, festivals etc., by the students (especially NSS students), NGO and social workers. Without peoples' participation (Starting from family the society) nothing is possible.

Mass media (Films, televisions, radios, theatres, and press) research organisations, NGOs, Trade Unions, government and political parties can play an important role in generating awareness regarding child labours at sectoral, organisational, local or national level.

It is easy to touch the organised sector but too difficult for the unorganised sector where more than 90 per cent of children are working. Here the responsibility of the NGOs, social workers and media are challenging.

References

1. Becerra, Rosina M. and Xiovanmon Jeanne M: *Defining Child Abuse* (Book).
2. Dek, Usha: *How Protected Indian Children are?*
3. Economic and Political Weekly Dec. 4, 1999, Editorial.
4. Goyal, R.S.: *Problems of Child Labour in India.*
5. Kanungo, Jyotirmayee: *Young Girls Helping Us in Our Household Works.*
6. Kar, Rabi Narayan: *Child Labour in India.*
7. Kumar, Dr. A. and Tripathy, S.K. *Child Labour in Orissa Strategies for their Rehabilitation.*
8. Kautilya: Arthashtra.
9. Mangia, Parveen: *Generating Awareness on Undesirable Aspects of Child Labour.*
10. Patel, S: *Concepts and Measures of Child Labour.*
11. Pattnaik, Raghunath: *Exploitation of Child Labour Law and some Random Facts.*
12. Ray: Dr. Dilip: *Child Labour—A Harsh Reality.*